OPENING
DOORS
WITHIN

EILEEN CADDY
*Edited and compiled
by David Earl Platts*

Copyright © Eileen Caddy 1986
Edited and compiled by David Earl Platts
First published 1987
Reprinted 8 Times

British Library Cataloguing-in-Publication Data. A catalogue
record for this book is available from the British Library.

Cased edition ISBN 0 905249 66 6
Paperback edition ISBN 0 905249 68 2

Illustrations by Claudia Klingemann
Cover illustration © Digital Stock 1999
Cover design by Thierry Bogliolo
Author photo by Findhorn Foundation Visual Arts

Printed by Interprint Ltd, Malta

Published by

Findhorn Press

The Park
Forres IV36 3TY
Scotland, UK
tel 01309 690582
fax 01309 690036
email books@findhorn.org

P. O. Box 13939
Tallahassee
Florida 32317-3939, USA
tel (850) 893 2920
fax (850) 893 3442
email info@findhornpress.com

findhornpress.com

In 1953 Eileen Caddy first began to receive personal guidance from a still, small voice deep within herself, from a source she calls the God within.

The simple teachings she has received over the years offer spiritual truth and vision, and insight into how to live a more happy, more meaningful, more fulfilling life. It has been her guidance which has served as the source of inspiration for the creation and development of what has become the Findhorn Foundation, the international spiritual community and holistic education centre in northern Scotland.

This is a book of spiritual values—love, joy, peace, gratitude, unity. You will find these and other themes echoing over and over again throughout the book, for, in the words of Eileen's guidance, 'Very gently and very lovingly I go on and on reminding you of the things that do matter in life until eventually they become a part of you, and live and move and have their being in you.'

This perennial diary offers inspirational messages of practical and compelling guidance in simple and direct prose, with specific suggestions for your daily spiritual growth and development.

You may wish to read each day's message upon awakening to provide an overall direction to your day. Or to have your family take turns reading it at the breakfast table. Or to use it as the basis for a daily meditation. And to re-read it at bedtime to help put your day in perspective.

However you choose to use them, take these teachings into yourself, and carry them with you day after day, year after year, until 'they become a part of you and live and move and have their being in you', until they have done their silent and gentle and loving work of 'Opening Doors Within'.

David Earl Platts

I was shown a bowl of food placed in the snow and I saw imprints of many birds and other animals around, as they knew they would find food there. I heard the words:

You cannot live by bread alone. Come to Me for your spiritual food and sustenance, and I will infil you and send you forth refreshed and renewed and fully satisfied.

LIFT up your heart and enter the new year with the knowledge that a truly wonderful year is there ahead of you. Behold the very best come forth out of everything. I can tell you what a glorious year it will be. But unless you accept what I say with a heart full of gratitude and expect the very best because your faith and trust are in My word, it will not come about. You have to help it come about. You have to hold on to My wonderful promises and believe. It is not a question of believing with your mind. You have to believe with the intuition, with that inner knowing which comes from the highest, from Me. Visualise Me going before you preparing the way, making the seemingly impossible become possible. Only the very, very best, the perfect, is for those souls who truly love Me and put Me first in everything.

BE not concerned if your beginnings into this spiritual life are small. All good things have small beginnings. The mighty oak starts from a tiny acorn. From a tiny seed the most wonderful plants and flowers spring forth. From a tiny seed of love many lives can be changed. From a tiny thought of faith and belief wonder upon wonder can come about. Little things grow into big things. Be grateful for all the little things in life; then, as they grow, you will be grateful for each and every one, and you will express your gratitude in words and deeds. Let that which is within express itself without. Always remember that a grateful heart is an open heart, and it is much easier for Me to work in and through an open heart. Give thanks and keep on giving thanks for everything, so I can work in and through you all the time and bring about My wonders and glories for all to see.

WHENEVER you love, love wholeheartedly, and never be afraid to show your love. Let your love be like an open book that all souls can read. It is the most wonderful thing in the world, so let that divine love within you flow freely. Love is not blind, but it sees the very best in the loved one, and so it draws forth the very best. Never pick and choose whom you are going to love. Simply keep your heart open and keep the love flowing to all souls alike. Doing so is loving with My divine love. It is like the sun and shines on all alike. Love should never be turned on and off like a tap. Love is never exclusive, never possessive. The more you are willing to share it, the greater it becomes. Hold on to it and you will lose it. Let go of it, and it returns to you a thousand-fold and becomes a joy and a blessing to all who share in it.

WHAT does it mean to you to live by faith? Where is your security? Is it in people? In your bank account? Or is it firmly rooted and grounded in Me, the Lord your God, the divinity within you? Take time to ponder on it, and you will know without a shadow of doubt exactly where your faith and security lie. Can you joyously and fearlessly take a big step in your life without any seeming outer security? When you know something is right, can you do it without hesitation? Can you confidently put your hand in Mine and say, 'Thy will be done,' and mean it with your whole heart and soul, and take that step into the unknown, willing to accept whatever comes? The only way to build up faith is by taking those small and even faltering steps and then bigger ones until your faith is so strong that you can take great leaps into the unknown because you know I AM with you always.

RE you willing to change? Take time to be still and then be very honest with yourself. Do you feel complacent and self-satisfied? Do you feel it is right for others to change, but your life is all right? If this is your attitude, it is time you had a real spring clean and turned your thinking, in fact the whole of your life, upside down and reviewed the contents. When you have done so, do not start putting back anything unless you are completely satisfied that it is of the highest and you do have need of it. The emptier you are, the better, because you then make room for the new to infil you. It is when you have nothing and feel completely empty that I can step in. Be not distressed when you feel bereft of everything. Call upon Me, and I will give you the kingdom. I withhold nothing from those souls who seek My help and guidance in true humility and love.

NEVER be envious of another's spiritual advancement or achievements. Realise that you too can do the same. But you have to do something about it and not just sit there bemoaning your lot in life. Every soul can reach the heights. Every soul can find direct contact with Me. Every soul can walk and talk with Me if you want to and accept the fact. You must believe it is possible and you must want to do it; then you most certainly will. It need not take lifetimes. It need not take any time. You can change in the twinkling of an eye if you choose to do so. One moment you can be walking in the old, and the next you can be in the glorious new. It can happen as quickly as that, with no effort at all on your part but a deep longing, determination, and absolute faith and belief. Why not try it, and let My peace and love infil and enfold you!

NEVER at any time close your heart and mind. Never be afraid of the new, of the strange, of the unconventional. Be ready and prepared to listen to the intuition, to inspiration which may reveal something so completely new to you that it may not even have form or substance, and you may have to clothe it in words. Intellectual pride can be a handicap along this spiritual path and can be a real stumbling block to the truth. It is not the intellect you need; it is inspiration and intuition. The intellect comes from without, whereas inspiration and intuition come from within and cannot be influenced by anything without. Let your learning come from within; draw from all that you have within you. You will be amazed at what you contain. It is limitless because it comes from Me and I AM limitless, and all that is of Me is limitless and eternal.

WHAT are you holding in your consciousness? I want only the very best, the very highest for you. If you choose of your own free will anything less and draw it towards you and are satisfied with second best, there is nothing I can do about it. Never be afraid to expect the best. Never feel you are unworthy or are not justified in having the best. I tell you it is your true heritage, but you have to claim it; you have to accept it and expect it. It is yours, My gift to you. Are you going to accept it with a full and grateful heart, or reject it? Let not false humility prevent you from accepting what is yours by rights; and do not just accept it, but glory in it, and give eternal thanks for it. Treasure it, and watch the wonder of it unfold in your life, knowing without a shadow of doubt that all I have is yours.

THOSE souls who abide in Me and live and move and having their being in My light and love are fully protected from all forces that would destroy. So be not bowed down by the cares of the world or by the conditions of your fellow human beings. If you become bowed down you cannot help, for you become part of the chaos and confusion that the world is in. As the darkness in the world grows ever denser, your inner light must increase in power and strength so that you can overcome the world and demonstrate eternal life and light. Allow nothing negative within you to dim the light, but let it blaze forth in you. The light within cannot be extinguished by any force without, but remains forever burning brightly, no matter what world conditions may be like. By your living example, you can help to change darkness into light. Keep in constant contact with me, letting Me inspire you in every way.

EARN to seek within for all the answers. Take time to be still, and find the answer in the silence. Never despair if it does not come immediately. Simply wait upon Me, and know that My timing is always perfect and in perfect rhythm with the whole of creation. How easy it is when life is not going very smoothly to throw up your hands in despair and try to run away from it all, instead of facing your responsibilities and allowing quietness and confidence to be your strength. Seek My will before all else. When you truly love Me, you will want to do My will, for love longs to do all for the Beloved. Therefore, when you hear My still small voice deep within you, follow through all I ask of you for your very love for Me. Know that I will never fail you nor forsake you. Know that only the very best will come out of all you do for My sake.

*T*HERE may be many paths, but the goal is the same in each. There is always the easy way or the hard way of reaching the goal. There is the direct route or the devious route which leads up highways and byways before getting there. The choice is always up to the individual. You are absolutely free to choose your own path. Therefore seek and follow it, even if in the end you realise how much time you have wasted taking the devious route when you could so easily have taken the direct one. Do you know where you are going and what you are doing? Do you know that you are in the right place and at peace within yourself? It is important that you search your own heart and find out, for you cannot give your very best when you do not feel you are in your rightful place doing what you know you should be doing with joy and love.

HEN a small child learning to walk falls down, it is not discouraged, but picks itself up and tries again and again until it has mastered the art of walking. So with the spiritual life. Never at any time allow seeming defeats to discourage you from advancing along the spiritual path. If you fall, simply pick yourself up and try again. Be not content to lie there in self-pity and say you cannot carry on and that life is too difficult. Your attitude must always be that of absolute inner certainty that once your feet have been set upon the spiritual path, you will reach the goal in the end, no matter what obstacles you may meet along the way. You will find time spent alone in the silence recharges you spiritually and helps you to face whatever is ahead without flinching or faltering. That is why time spent alone with Me each morning helps to fortify you for whatever the day may bring.

ITHOUT faith you cannot travel this spiritual path. Without trust there is no love; and without love life is empty. Open your heart and keep the love flowing, no matter how difficult life may appear to be on the surface. Rise above your outer conditions and circumstances into those realms where all is light, all is peace, all is perfection, and there is no separation. You have to make the choice to do it, and then you have to do it. Allow nothing from without to depress you. See that glorious silver lining behind every dark cloud, and concentrate on it until the cloud is no more. Learn to soar like a lark, up, up into the heights, singing songs of praise and thanksgiving. Be not anchored to the ways of the world, to the materialism in life. It is the ways of the Spirit that matter. Start right now to live by the Spirit and walk in the ways of the Spirit.

HERE are so many wonderful things to do in life, but what can you do best? Find out and then go ahead and do it and enjoy doing it. Do not waste time and energy longing to do something else, or wishing you were somewhere else with other opportunities. Realise you are in exactly the right place at the right time, and you are there for a specific purpose to do a specific job. Therefore give all you have to that job, and do it with love and joy. See what fun life can be, not just for yourself, but also for all those souls around you. Unless you give of your very best to the whole, you cannot hope to become part of that whole. You cut yourself off from it, and there is no wholeness in you. What deep satisfaction you will find when you do what has to be done perfectly and you do it for the benefit of the whole!

WHY not relax? Let go and let Me take over, for the more stress and strain there is in your life, the less you get done. Why not let yourself flow with nature, flow with the tide, and do what has to be done quite simply, naturally and joyously? Why not enjoy life, instead of going through it with grim determination, forcing yourself to do this, that and the other without any joy or love? Life is wonderful when you are in harmony with it and cease resisting anything. Why make everything complicated for yourself? Why not make today a special day, and see the very best in everything? Give thanks for everything. Enjoy everything as it should be enjoyed. I want you to enjoy life. Start off by seeing the beauty of nature all around you, and you will find that one wonderful thing will lead to the next, until your whole life is one of wonderment and joy.

IF ever you are in any doubt about some action to be taken, why not be still and wait upon Me, and never rush ahead and do something without My blessing. Always know where you are going, and you will not get lost on the way; that is why it is important to wait until I give you the green light before you go ahead. It is not wasting time to be still and wait upon Me. It saves so much time in the end when you do the right thing, rather than when you rush ahead and do the wrong thing, and then have to retrace your steps and undo all you have done by your unguided impetuosity. When you know that something is right, then do not hesitate to see it through immediately. It is when there is that slight feeling of uncertainty over anything that you must wait, wait, wait, until things clarify for you before taking action.

LIFE without prayer is empty and meaningless, for it is that communion with the higher part of you which reveals to you the fullness of this glorious life which is your true heritage. Let your prayers be very positive and constructive, and give thanks for what you are about to receive, even before you pray for it. As you pray, feel a oneness, a unity in all life where there is no separation, for all is one. Prayer unites all; it draws all together and creates perfect oneness. Talk to Me and listen to Me. Never waste time in beseeching Me for this, that and the other, for that is not true prayer. To beseech is to create separateness, and I want you to create oneness at all times. We are one. I AM within you; you do not have to search for Me without. I AM always here waiting for you to recognise Me. Recognise our oneness now; I in you, and you in Me.

IT is up to you to make today the most wonderful day you have ever lived, by your right attitude, by your positive thought. See today as My day, a day fully blessed by Me, and see it all unfold for you in true perfection, with never a thought of disappointment to mar it. Why should you be disappointed at anything today may bring? Remember that you are in full control of it. You are master of the situation; therefore it is up to you how it unfolds. If you are faced with a problem, know there is an answer to it, and never allow the problem to get you down. See it as a stepping stone; see it as a challenge, and the solution will reveal itself. Never, never allow the problem to control you. You have to do it. You have to make the effort to think positively, to think big, to think success. Then watch it come about step by step.

*Y*OU cannot hope to grow spiritually unless you are prepared to change. Those changes may come in small ways to begin with, but as you move further and further into the new, they will become more drastic and vital. Sometimes it needs a complete upheaval to bring about a whole new way of life. But it is amazing how soon you can get used to change as long as you have the courage and conviction that the changes which are taking place are all for the very best. Let perfection always be your aim. Keep stretching. Keep reaching up to the seemingly impossible. Keep growing in wisdom and understanding, and never at any time be content to remain static. There is always something more to be learnt. There is always something new and wonderful to discover in this life, so expand your consciousness and your imagination to make room for it. Keep open and receptive so that you miss nothing.

LL I have is yours when you learn to put first things first, but you must take time and search your heart and know what you are putting first in your life. Remember, you can hide nothing from Me, so be completely frank and honest with yourself. Does your work for Me mean more to you than anything, or are you inclined to push it into the background, and only do My will when you feel like it and it suits you? If so, you are not putting first things first. Only when everything is surrendered to Me can I work freely in and through you to bring about My wonders and glories. Let not your surrender be half-hearted or fearful. When you give anything, give it whole-heartedly and with real love and joy, and have no regrets whatsoever. Know that I will use your gift in the way it should be used, to My honour and glory and for the benefit of the whole.

START the day by giving thanks. Realise that you are mightily blessed and that My blessings are being poured down upon you all the time. It does not matter how ungrateful you were yesterday; what matters is what your attitude is now. Leave the past behind. Do not waste time concentrating on your past mistakes; simply learn from them and then move on and enjoy life, giving constant thanks for everything. When you are grateful and you appreciate all the good things in life, love flows freely in and through you. It is when you fail to give thanks and to appreciate all My good and perfect gifts that you grow dry and brittle. You become self-concerned and cease to care for your fellow human beings. The quickest way to change this wrong attitude is to start thinking for others and to start living and giving to the whole. You will find the self and self-concern will melt into the background and become as nothing. Why not do it now?

TOP freewheeling, get into gear, and do something with your life. There are many avenues to explore, so why not explore them? Never be afraid to step out into the unknown, into the new. Do it fearlessly, always expecting the very best as you do so. Life is very thrilling and exciting, but you must be willing to branch out into the new in absolute faith and trust. Let Me be your constant guide and companion. There is much waiting to be revealed to you when you are ready. You must be properly equipped for this life of adventure. You have to learn vitally important lessons before you venture forth. You have to learn those fundamental lessons of obedience and discipline. It is why you have to be tried and tested. Do not be impatient when you have to go through these tests and trials, but be grateful that you have been chosen to follow this spiritual path.

WHY put off until later something that is your divine heritage now? I AM within you, closer than breathing, nearer than hands and feet. Can you accept it? Or do you still have doubts and wonder if it is possible? It is something all individuals have to work out for themselves. They can be told it over and over again, but until they are willing to accept it as fact, and to know the wonder of it, it means nothing to them. Or it is just a lovely dream that perhaps one day may become reality. What time is wasted in doubting and disbelief! It is only when you know the truth that the truth sets you free. Hearing about it, talking about it, or reading about it does not do it. The truth has to live and move and have its being within you. Then it does set you free, and you know the true meaning of freedom of heart, mind and spirit.

CEASE looking to others for help and look for it within, and you will find it. Always go to the Source for the answer, and do not be satisfied with anything second-hand, or anything that is not of the very highest. By starting from the bottom and working upward, you will be cleansed and purified throughout and can start off with solid rock-like foundations which nothing and no one can shake or destroy. Once your foundations are sound, you can go on building and building without any concern. See that your foundations are rooted and grounded in Me, in the ways of the Spirit, and not in the ways of the world which are here today and gone tomorrow. Live and move and have your whole being in Me. Let My peace and love infil and enfold you. Lift up your heart in deep love, praise and gratitude, and be at perfect peace as you do My will and walk in My ways.

ET there be no wishful thinking in this spiritual life. It is a very real, practical life, a life full of excitement and expectancy. Expect the impossible to become possible. Expect miracle upon miracle to come about simply because you are living and demonstrating My divine laws. When you live by My laws, anything can happen at any time because you are in tune with the higher powers and are working from a higher level of consciousness. You are at one with the Universal Mind, with Me. When there is no separation and we are working as one, all things are possible. So get into tune. Start the day by getting into tune with Me, by being still and finding that inner peace and serenity which nothing can destroy. A sensitive musical instrument has to be tuned before it can be played. How much more do you have to be tuned each day before you enter and play your part in the orchestra of life?

OU cannot create the new by remaining immersed in the old. A newborn babe cannot remain attached to its mother. The umbilical cord has to be cut so that it becomes a separate being. So with this spiritual life. Once you have set your foot on the spiritual path and have decided to live in the ways of the Spirit, you have to make a clean break with your old way of life. You cannot have a foot in both worlds. The choice is yours. Let there be no going back on that choice. Keep moving forward. It is when the going is rough that you may crave the so-called 'good old days' and want to go back. There is no going back in this life. A babe cannot return to its mother's womb when life becomes too hard for it. A chick cannot return to its shell, or a butterfly to its chrysalis. Life cannot go backwards. It has to go forward, always forward.

DO you realise that what you do, how you live and how you think can help or hinder the state of the world? Cease being drawn into the whirlpool of chaos and confusion, of destruction and devastation, and start right now concentrating on the wonder and beauty of the world around you. Give thanks for everything. Bless all those souls whom you contact. Refuse to see the worst in people, in things or in conditions, and seek always for the very best. It is not being like an ostrich hiding your head in the sand and refusing to face the realities of the world. It is simply looking for and concentrating on the very best in everything and everyone. You are a tiny world within yourself. When there is peace, harmony, love and understanding right there deep within your little world, it will be reflected in the outer world all around you. When you can do it, you are beginning to help the whole vast situation in the world.

HY not try listening to those inner intangible sounds which can only be heard in absolute stillness when you become in tune with the ways of the Spirit? In that state of perfect peace your whole life changes, and a deep inner tranquillity and serenity are radiated from within. You become one with the whole of life. You feel uplifted, inspired and filled with illumination, for your whole being is filled with My divine light. You understand not with the mind, but with the higher consciousness and with the heart. You are no longer living unto yourself. The self is completely forgotten, and your life is one of giving love and service to your fellow human beings. It is only when you are giving that you find the wonderful inner joy and happiness which nothing and no one can take from you. Joy comes with service, and service comes with dedication. Dedicate yourself to Me and to My service now, and feel yourself expand as you do so.

RE you ready to change your ideas and change your thinking? Are you prepared to accept something new without reservations? Some souls can be flexible and do it with the greatest of ease, but others have great difficulty, and it causes strain and stress in their lives. Or it causes stagnation—which is almost as bad. You must be courageous and move forward into new ways, new and even uncharted waters, without any fear. I AM guiding you into those new and uncharted waters, and I will not let any harm befall you. Accept Me as your constant guide and companion. You have not been asked to move into those uncharted waters without your pilot. I AM your pilot, and I will never let you down. Trust Me completely. If the way is rough, be not afraid; if it is dangerous, be not concerned. I will guide you through it all. But remember to let go and let Me do it, and resist not.

DO you find real joy in the work you are doing and in the life you are living? Do you find real pride in a job not only well done, but perfectly done? Do you dislike anything that is done shoddily or half-heartedly? Is your heart so much in what you are doing and are you so conscious of the fact that you are doing everything to Me and to My honour and glory that you cannot be satisfied with anything that is not 'just so'? It is as it should be. You should never be satisfied with a job done in a half-hearted, begrudging manner. Do all that has to be done with joy and love, and let it include everything you do, from the most mundane job to those vitally important ones. See that your attitude is right in everything you undertake so that the right vibrations are put into it. What is more, you will find yourself enjoying it.

RAISE your consciousness and realise you are ageless. You are as young as time, as old as eternity. As you live fully and gloriously in the ever present now, you are always as young as the present. You are constantly being reborn in Spirit and in truth. You cannot remain static in this spiritual life; there is always something new and exciting to learn and to do. Living in a state of expectancy keeps you ever alert and young. It is when the mind becomes old and dull that life loses all its sparkle and zest. When you fail to understand some new truth with the mind, sit still and raise your consciousness, get into tune with the infinite Universal Mind and become one with it, with Me, and you will be able to understand all things. Keep your mind alert and you can never grow old. The fountain of youth is your consciousness; the joy of living is the elixir of life.

I was shown a very rough and angry sea with mountainous waves. Then I saw that below the surface was a wonderful peace and stillness. I heard the words:

Seek and find that peace which passes all understanding deep within, and retain it, no matter what is happening without.

WHAT do you believe in? Do you believe in Me? Do you believe that you can walk and talk with Me? Do you believe, when you live this spiritual life fully integrated and at one with Me, that it works, that it is a very practical life, and that there is nowhere in your life where this way of life does not work? Take time to sort out and weigh up your beliefs, and above all, learn to live by them. Far too many souls fail to put into practice this way of life. They talk about it but have not yet proved to themselves and to the world that it does work and that when you recognise Me in everything and call upon Me and seek My help, everything starts to fall into place in your life. When you obey My still, small voice within, you begin to unfold like a beautiful flower and you see what a truly practical, wonderful life it is.

THERE is much to be done, but you must learn to channel your energies in the right direction and not fritter them away by dabbling in many activities. It is easy to do, so here is where self-discipline is necessary. You have to find what you should be doing, and then go straight ahead and not be tempted to try your hand at a hundred and one different tasks. You need variety and you need to be flexible, but it does not mean to dissipate your energy. It is far better to learn to do one thing and to do it perfectly than to indulge in many things and do them badly. I ask you not to be a dabbler in the many, but to be a perfectionist in everything you undertake. Be willing to learn and never feel that you know all the answers. There is always something new to learn. Learn to do what you know you can do perfectly. Let your standards be of the very highest.

AS you follow My laws and obey them, your life becomes rich and mightily blessed. Disobey these laws, and sooner or later you will find yourself slipping downhill, until you realise where you have gone wrong and are determined to rectify those wrongs. It is when you have to start putting first things first and when you have to turn away from your waywardness and seek Me and My kingdom. It is not easy to do when you have reached rock-bottom and feel there is no purpose in life. Yet it is what you will have to do. Put your feet on the bottom rung of the ladder and start climbing, no matter how difficult it may appear at the time. As you pull yourself up to the next rung and gradually work your way out of the despair you have sunk into, life will begin to change for you and you will find a real purpose in your life and living.

*T*O live a spiritual life does not mean you are deprived of all those worldly goods you have need of and that make life easier. It simply means that you have the use of every single thing you need to use for the benefit of the whole and to My honour and glory. When you have finished with it, whatever it may be, it is returned to Me with love and gratitude, because you recognise that all you have is Mine. You will find the more you give away, the more room there is for more to enter. Accept all that you need, but never try to possess it. The more possessive you are of anything, the more likely you are to lose it. My store-houses are full to overflowing. As you get your values right, you will lack absolutely nothing. But always remember to put Me first in everything, to give thanks for everything, and to return to Me that which you have finished with.

HEN you are given responsibilities to carry, shoulder them joyously and be not bowed down by them. See that they are carried out to the letter, and never fail to see them through, no matter how seemingly difficult or heavy they may appear to be at the time. Always remember that I never give you more than you are able to carry without giving you the help and strength to do it. As you shoulder your responsibilities, you grow in stature and strength and become dependable and reliable so that I can give you even greater responsibilities to carry. I need more and more reliable and dependable souls to carry the load. I need you willing and able to do it without any fear of not being able to do it. Never at any time be a defeatist. You can do anything when you make up your mind you can, and refuse even to contemplate failure. Simply know that you will succeed, and you will.

B E guided in all that you do and say. Learn to be very patient and to wait for the right timing for everything. Know that all things will work out perfectly when you wait upon Me and do not rush ahead unguidedly. Much is waiting to unfold at the right time. Everything is being speeded up, but nevertheless it will be an unfolding process which will take place, for there is perfect harmony and rhythm in My plan. Nothing is out of step, so work with it and not against it. If you try to work against it, you will simply exhaust yourself and will get nowhere, and it will be like swimming against the tide. You will either remain stationary by swimming with all your strength, or you will be swept back with the force of the tide. Avoid working against something which is inevitable, but instead learn to go along with it in absolute peace and confidence that you are doing the right thing at the right time.

AKE time to search your heart. Are you taking anything or anyone for granted? Do you ever feel bored and fed up with life? Are you a giver or a taker? Is your life one of service to your fellow human beings, or do you demand certain rights for yourself? You cannot expect to find true and lasting happiness unless you give, and are there to serve without any demand for the self in any way. Only when you can accept that this life is a life of service, a life of giving, a life of complete dedication to Me and in My service, a life where the self is forgotten and you are living for the whole, can you understand what I mean when I say that it is indeed a full and glorious life you are living and how mightily blessed you are. So start right now expanding your consciousness. Start living and working for the whole, and see how your entire outlook and attitude will change.

WAKE refreshed and renewed, expecting the very best from the glorious day and therefore receiving only the very best. Relax and let Me take over. Never start the day strained and full of tension. Sleep and rest renew the Spirit and revitalise it. Start the day off on the right foot with a heart full of love and gratitude, full of great expectations for the new day. Today has no blemishes on it to mar it, so why not keep it that way? Keep your consciousness raised to the highest and see the most wonderful happenings unfold this day. It is a new day and a new way. Leave yesterday behind with all its faults and failings, and turn over a new page. Why drag the old behind you into this new day? By all means learn your lessons, but why dwell so much on those lessons that they drag you down so that you cannot enter the new with a light and joyous heart?

HE new heaven and new earth are here now. It is simply a question of recognising and accepting what is happening and raising your consciousness so that you are fully aware of all that is taking place within and around you. If you are not aware of all that is taking place at this time, it does not mean it is not happening. It simply means you have shut it out by your own pride and arrogance which have blinded you to the wonders all around you. Therefore keep raising your consciousness. The higher you raise it, the more clearly can you see the truth, and there is nothing in the way to blot out the full vision. When you have beheld the wonder of that vision, then bring it down and live it; let it become part of your everyday living. Unless a vision is manifested in form, it does not become reality. I tell you to behold My new heaven and new earth manifested in form now.

*A*IM high; the higher, the better. Even if you do not achieve that high aim every time, at least you will find yourself being stretched to capacity. Always expect the very best in life; see yourself receiving it; and give eternal thanks for it. Remember that I know what you have need of, even before you ask, and all your needs are being wonderfully met. How blessed you are to know these wonderful truths and to be able to absorb them into the very depths of your being! To be aware of the tremendous changes and the constant growth and expansion on all levels. To know that with all the upheavals in the world which are bound to come, for the old must go to make room for the new, no harm will befall those souls who have learnt to put their whole faith and trust in Me. To know without a shadow of a doubt that with Me all things are possible.

UNTIL you are willing to give of yourself to Me and take time to be still and get into tune with Me, I have no channel to work in and through. Always remember, you have to do your part. You have to put first things first, and as you do so, you open up all doors, and I AM able to work wonder upon wonder in and through you. Without channels, My work is held up. I need more and more channels cleared of the self so there is nothing to stop the free flow in and through you. I cannot use you unless you give of yourself. I never take anything unless it is freely given. So give your all to Me, withhold nothing, and forget the self completely in your giving. Get into rhythm with life, into rhythm with Me, and flow with ease and grace. Waste no more time thinking about it, but do something about it now.

EE a perfect pattern and plan running through your life. There is nothing haphazard. Even though it may appear to be very strange, all is in My divine plan. You would not be where you are, doing what you are doing at this time, if I had not laid My hand upon you. My ways are not your ways. Seek always to do My will. I know what is best for you, so why fight against it and think that you know best? Have absolute faith and trust in Me. Know that I AM always here and that I will never let you down or forsake you. Keep turning to Me. Listen to what I have to say to you in the silence and obey My slightest whisper. Obedience opens up a whole new life for you and releases new energies which have been hidden deep within you waiting to be released when you are ready and willing to follow them without question.

RAW from the infinite source of power and strength within, and you will find yourself doing seemingly supernatural things simply because you are working with My divine laws. Anything can happen, for My laws are the keys that open all doors and make all things possible. Recognise them as My laws, and never fail to give eternal thanks for them, and use them to My honour and glory and for the benefit of the whole. Then only the most wonderful happenings can come out of their right use, and all shall benefit from them. Power used aright under My guidance can change the course of history, creating the new heaven and new earth. Used wrongly, it can bring only devastation and destruction. Power is something that must not be played with, but must be treated with great respect. I AM power. I hold all creation in My hand, and you are part of that whole. Blend with it, and find your rightful place in it.

OVE is in the air. Feel the warmth of it, the joy of it, and the freedom that comes with it. Love is an inner state of being. It does not have to be talked about, for it expresses itself in a thousand and one little ways: a look, a touch, an action. Love is everywhere, but you have to be aware of it to appreciate it fully. The air you breathe is everywhere, but you take it all for granted unless you stop and become aware of it and of the fact that it keeps you alive. Take nothing for granted, for when you do, it takes all the joy and sparkle out of life. Love starts with small beginnings and grows and grows. When you truly love one another, you have faith and trust in each other. Keep that love flowing and let nothing stand in the way. Let My divine love flow through everything, and know that peace which passes all understanding.

THE secret of making anything work is to want to make it work, and to be so positive about it that it could not possibly do otherwise. To tackle any difficult job in a half-hearted way does not call for success; but when it is tackled whole-heartedly and with a real desire to see it work, only the very best will come about. Let everything you undertake be undertaken whole-heartedly, from the very smallest and mundane job to the most difficult and complicated ones. Be willing to accept real challenges in life, and never be afraid of them. When they are faced in the right spirit and with the inner knowledge that it is I working in and through you who will help you to accomplish the task, anything can happen. Change your outlook, and you can open the door to an inflow of very positive and creative energies to your whole being. Realise you can change and change at great speed, but it is up to you.

WHAT are you doing about the things that matter in life? Have you got your values right? Why not take time to be still, go into the silence, study your motives, and see whether they are of the highest? Only you can do it. No one else can do it for you. It may even mean waiting upon Me without receiving an immediate answer. You may have important lessons to learn which you can learn only by being still and waiting upon Me, especially if you are an impatient and demanding soul. Why make excuses for yourself? You know all the answers in theory. Now it is time you put them into practice and see how they work for you. You will never learn these vitally important lessons until you put them to the test yourself. Why not do it now and stop wasting time thinking about them? Learn to get your values right and put first things first. Let Me work in and through you.

WHEN you are willing to surrender your all to Me and hold nothing back, then your every need will be wonderfully met and your life will flow with abundance, for you open the flood gates when you surrender all to Me. Absorb this law into your whole being until it becomes part of you and you vibrate with that rhythm of all life and know the meaning of wholeness, of being in tune with the whole of creation, and therefore in tune with Me. I AM the creator of all creation; I AM the wholeness of all life. Raise your consciousness, and realise that I AM within you, that this wholeness is here within you, and that nothing can separate you from the wonder of it except your own limited consciousness. Why not let go and let it expand? Allow nothing to stop that expansion of consciousness until you can accept that I AM in you, and you are in Me, and we are One.

W HEN you pour forth love and understanding, they will come back to you a hundredfold. When you pour forth criticism and negativity, so shall they be returned to you a hundredfold. That which is deep within you will be reflected in your life without. You cannot hide your discontent, your dislike or your misery, for sooner or later they will erupt on the outer like a boil, and then it will have to be lanced. The sooner the poison is dispersed, the better. The best and the quickest way of doing it is to change your whole attitude. Replace those poisonous, negative, critical thoughts with thoughts of purest love, harmony and understanding. It can be done at great speed. You do not have to wallow in your misery and depression. You do not have to waste precious time being sorry for yourself. When you want to do something about your situation, you can do it immediately. Change can come in the twinkling of an eye.

HERE are very important lessons which have to be learnt by everyone in this life. For example, learn to do what has to be done quietly and unobtrusively and without any noise or fanfare. Do not sweep such lessons aside or think you know all the answers and therefore you do not have to learn such elementary lessons. Look deep within and let not spiritual pride blind you to your shortcomings, for you cannot be fully used when you allow spiritual pride to stand in the way. So often pride can prevent you from learning new and vitally important lessons which are waiting to be learnt, and it can stunt your spiritual growth. There is always something new and wonderful to learn and absorb, and you will only be able to do it when you are willing to keep open and realise your need. Seek to meet that need in true humility and deep gratitude. You never stop learning in this life.

WHY be afraid of anything? I AM with you always. I go before you to prepare the way; and it will unfold in true perfection at the right time. You must have faith, and your faith must be strong and rocklike to be able to live this life. Your faith grows stronger when it is put into practice. Faith is not something to be talked about. It has to be lived so that all souls can see that it is not some glorious state of living up in the clouds, but is very real and is something that works in everyday living. It is quite useless to talk about faith or read about it if you do not live by it. It means you have to step off the deep end and swim, not just paddle around in the shallows with your foot on the bottom, pretending to yourself that you can swim. Why not get into action and live this full and glorious life now?

N O one likes to be hurt or slighted; no one likes to be ignored or made to feel unloved and unwanted. So why not treat your fellow human beings with love and respect? Try to understand them and be willing to go that second mile with them if necessary. Be very tolerant, very patient and very loving. It is the way you would like to be treated yourself, so live as you would wish others to live. Be a good example, but never do it because you feel it is expected of you. Do it because you want to do it and long with all your heart to give of your best in everything you do, say and think. The greater your desire, the easier it will be to fulfil it. Never be satisfied with anything mediocre or half-hearted. See that everything you do is of the very highest, that your motives are pure, and that there is nothing selfish or self-centred in anything you do.

E yourself, and do not try to be like anyone else. It takes all sorts to make a world. I do not want you all alike, like peas in a pod. I need you all different, each doing your specific job and playing your specific part, blending in perfectly with the whole. It does not mean that there need be any disharmony or discord because you are all different. There are many different musical instruments in a full orchestra, and each has its rightful place in the whole and blends in perfectly when working in harmony with the whole. It is when individual souls go off on their own tangents with no thought or consideration for the whole that discord and chaos are created. When your heart is in the right place and you are living and working together for the good of the whole, only the very best will come forth. Therefore cease struggling and let go. All you have to do is to be, and let everything unfold.

THE more you receive, the more you have to give. Hold nothing to the self, but give and give and go on giving, and so make room for more and more to infil you. The more aware you are of the changes which are taking place, and the more open you are to them, the faster can they come about. They become a part of you and you become a part of them. The ground has been prepared and the seeds have been sown. Now is the time of growing, expanding and flowering, and this process is what is taking place at this time. Behold the wonder and beauty of it all! See more and more souls awaken and become aware of what is happening. There is a tremendous surge forward. The ways of the Spirit are beginning to be a living reality to the many. Live by the Spirit, walk in the ways of the Spirit, and become one with all life.

WHAT is right for one soul may not be right for another. That is why it is important that you seek your own inner direction and act on it without trying to follow in anyone else's footsteps. You have free choice, for I have given all human beings free will. You are not like a puppet that cannot move without having the strings pulled. You can seek and find what is right for you, and then it is up to you what you do about it. You only find real peace of heart and mind when you follow what you know is right for you, so seek and go on seeking until you have found your specific way and then follow it. It may mean having to stand on your own and do something strange in the eyes of others, but be not daunted. Do whatever it is because you know within that it is right for you and that only the very best will come out of it.

SEE every difficulty as a challenge, a stepping stone, and never be defeated by anything or anyone. Keep moving forward, and know that the answer will be revealed to you when you are persistent and persevere. Be strong and of good courage, knowing that you will get there, come what may. There is no turning back at this stage. All the doors have been locked and barred behind you, so you must move forward. Time is getting short, and there is much to be done. You have your part to play in the overall plan. Find your rightful place in it, for when you know where you fit in, you can be at peace and can do what has to be done in complete confidence. It is a wonderful plan, a glorious one, so have no fear as you take part in it. Simply give of your very best and so help to fulfil it as quickly as possible, and watch it unfold in true perfection.

HERE are times when the new unfolds so gradually that you are not aware of the changes which are taking place until you suddenly realise it has all happened without your being aware of it. At other times you can see the changes taking place in front of your eyes as they unfold step by step. Then there are times when things happen overnight—rather as in winter, when you go to bed at night and the world outside is normal, and when you wake up in the morning, everything is covered with snow. You have not had to do a thing about it; it has all happened in the most miraculous way. There are many different ways in which the new will be revealed. All you have to do is go along with it and not resist it. Change need not be painful. It is inevitable because nothing can remain the same; and if you look into your heart, you would not want it to do so.

*Y*OU must recognise your freedom so that you can soar to great heights spiritually. Otherwise, you are like a bird in a cage, which, even though the door of the cage is wide open and it is free to fly where it will, fails to recognise its freedom and goes on fluttering about in its cage getting nowhere. You can go through the whole of your life like that bird, completely blind and in bondage, unless you recognise that you are free and accept your freedom and use it as it should be used, in the realms of the Spirit where there are no limitations, boundaries and barriers to hold you back. All human beings are free if only they would recognise it and accept it. That freedom is being held out to you, but you have to accept it before you can use it. Why not accept your freedom now, realising that you are bound to no one and nothing, and that you are capable of doing anything you desire?

ET go and let yourself inhabit that kingdom which is come but is waiting to be recognised and claimed by more and more souls. You pray that My kingdom come, My will be done on earth; now cease praying for it and claim it. Prayers without faith are empty. You must learn to pray believing with all your heart, mind and soul, so that your prayers, whatever they are, are very real and concrete, and you know without any doubt that they are being answered. Limit nothing. There is no limitation in My kingdom, and My kingdom is come, and in My kingdom all things are possible. Learn to live beyond yourself and your very human limitations. Live in the realms of the Spirit where you can do all things in Me. I strengthen and uphold you, so know that I AM with you always. How can it be otherwise, for I AM within you.

VERY soul needs to withdraw from the world from time to time to find the peace which passes all understanding. Every soul needs to be stabilised, and it can only come about in peace and stillness. Once that inner stability has been established, you can go anywhere and do anything without outer chaos and confusion affecting you in any way. Do you enjoy being still, or are you uncomfortable in the stillness? Does it make you squirm to find yourself in the silence, and do you long for noise and action all around you? Do you always want to be busy doing things, and find great difficulty in stilling your body and mind? There are millions of souls in the world who cannot bear silence; they have to have constant noise and action around them. They are restless within and without. I tell you, times of peace and stillness are very precious in a world of turmoil. Seek them, find them and remain in them.

I was shown a windmill. A strong wind was blowing, and the sails were turning at great speed. Then the wind dropped and the sails stopped turning, for they were completely dependent upon the wind for their movement. I heard the words:

Put not your security in the things of this life, but put your security in Me, the source of all power and strength deep within you.

XPECT a miracle. Expect miracle upon miracle to come about, and do not limit in any way. The more open you are, the better, for then there is nothing in the way to stop the flow of My laws, for miracles are simply My laws in action. Flow with those laws, and anything can happen! See the perfection of My plan unfold. There is no sense of rush or hurry. When something unfolds, it can unfold at great speed, but it does so with a great sense of peace and serenity, perfect timing and precision. Be afraid of nothing, for there is nothing to fear when your faith and trust are in Me. I AM within you, so see the perfection of My plan come about within you and without. It all starts from within and works its way without; therefore let nothing in you hinder its progress. Let it all come, and behold the new heaven and new earth.

MANY souls talk about faith, but fail to live by it. Those same souls talk about loving Me, but do not know the first thing about love. It is a waste of time talking about loving someone you have not seen, when you are incapable of loving those souls you have all around you and who need your love, wisdom and understanding. First learn to love those souls whom I have placed in your immediate surroundings; then you will know what it means to love Me truly. Why grope your way through life when all you have to do is to stride firmly through it in faith and confidence, knowing that I AM with you? Here I AM, holding out to you all My good and perfect gifts, but if you will not accept them, you cannot benefit from them. Freely I give them to you; freely you have to accept them, and then use them wisely for the benefit of the whole.

*Y*OU must be prepared for wonderful changes to take place in the New Age. If you can accept them and simply absorb them like a piece of blotting paper, the changes will come about within and around you in great peace and harmony. You will find that you will change with the changes without being unduly affected by them and that you will live and move and breathe in them as naturally as a fish does in water. You will be able to accept your new environment and become perfectly adjusted to it without any strain. A child moves from kindergarten to primary and from primary to secondary school without any difficulty because it takes it all in its stride and moves forward step by step, accepting each new subject and adjustment as it comes. It could not be moved straight from kindergarten to secondary, for it would be completely lost. Do not be concerned; I will not move you too swiftly. All is in My perfect timing.

WHAT a lot of time and energy are wasted because you do not take the time or trouble to be still and wait upon Me! It is the secret solution to every situation. Why not prove it to yourself by putting it into practice to see how it works? Until you try something and put it to the test, it remains a theory. This life is a very real, very practical life, a life of action. There is nothing theoretical about it, but it is up to you to do something about it to prove that it is so. The daylight is there, but until you pull back the curtains, you remain in darkness. Water is in the tap, but until you turn on the tap and let the water flow, it remains static. Food can be sitting there on your plate, but until you put it into your mouth and eat it, it does you no good. So get into action and do it now.

THINK wholeness, be wholeness, and manifest wholeness in your life. To be a whole person, you need to know yourself, know where you are going and know what you are doing, and then go ahead in confidence and live a whole, glorious and full life. Never have any doubts about yourself or your ability to be whole. It is doubts and fears and worries that prevent you from establishing wholeness; so cease your worrying, and banish all fears and doubts, in the knowledge that I AM with you always and that with Me all things are possible. But remember, always let your faith and confidence be in Me, the Lord your God, the divinity within you. Walk hand in hand with Me; consult Me at all times; and let Me guide and direct you. I AM within you, therefore nothing from without can interfere with our direct contact. Feel safe and secure in this knowledge. When your security is in Me, all is indeed very, very well.

*Y*OU can only think one thought at a time. Therefore see that that thought is constructive, positive and loving, and then you will find yourself saying constructive things and acting in a loving way. In fact, your whole outlook will be positive, and your life will be filled with love, joy, happiness, health, success and harmony. When you are at all sensitive and you have negative and destructive thoughts, they undermine your whole being. Your outlook becomes dimmed, and you feel depressed and even physically ill. Try to understand that you bring this state on yourself by your wrong thinking. Change it and you will change everything. You may imagine that you are surrounded by many difficulties and that your whole situation is to blame for your negative state of mind, but is it? Aren't your thoughts your own? Aren't you free to raise your consciousness and think loving, positive, constructive thoughts that create your well-being? The choice always lies in your hands.

*Y*OU cannot hope to create peace and harmony in the world until you have found peace and harmony within. You have to start with yourself. You have to start in a small way and let it grow and expand. A mighty oak tree has its beginnings in a tiny acorn, and yet within that tiny acorn it contains everything. You contain the peace of the world within you, so why not let it grow and expand within until it no longer can be contained and bursts forth, bringing peace and harmony into the world? It starts within you, so be consciously aware of the vitally important part which you have to play to help bring peace and harmony into the world. Never stand back and blame anyone else for the state of the world, but get into action and do something about it yourself. Now, be at perfect peace as you do My will and walk in My ways, glorifying Me.

*Y*OU are in this world to bring good into it. You are here to radiate love, light and wisdom to all those souls in need. You have work to do, and you can do this work only when you have sorted yourself out and can become one with the whole, when you no longer stand apart and criticise and separate yourself from the whole. Do you feel at one with all those souls around you? Do you feel at peace with the world, or are your thoughts conflicting, critical and destructive? Always remember, love, joy and happiness create the right atmosphere and draw all those souls of like mind together. So watch yourself, and start right now drawing only the very best to you. You can change your whole attitude and outlook in the twinkling of an eye. Why not do it? Get into tune with all life, and find that peace which passes all understanding.

AS you learn to give to others in service, it opens your heart and keeps it open. The more you give freely and joyously, the more love pours forth from you and the more love you draw to you. The more love you give, the more you will receive. It is the law. Never be discouraged if love is not returned to you immediately. Simply know that sooner or later it will be, and so keep the love flowing because love never takes 'no' for an answer. Love is never defeated. Love is not like a snail; it never withdraws when it is rebuffed or rejected. It turns the other cheek and goes on and on loving. Can you do it? You cannot do it on your own strength, but with Me you can do anything. Seek My help at all times and I will never fail you. You will find you can love and love and go on loving without any difficulty.

WHY not use what is yours to use? What is the use of having an electric light in your room if you fail to switch it on and fill the room with light? Why not keep turning to Me for help and strength, and use all those wonderful gifts which are there waiting for you? Cease struggling on your own, for when you know Me and love Me, you will want to be ever aware of Me and of My divine presence. You will want to walk in the light, for where there is light, darkness is no more. You generate light by your positive, constructive living and being; therefore allow nothing negative in you to dim that light. You may need to do it consciously until all negativity falls away from you and you learn to live positively all the time. It may be a real effort for you to do it to begin with, but gradually it will become as natural to you as breathing.

ORK with My laws, not against them. When you work against them you are fighting a losing battle and will get nowhere. When there is tension in you, seek within and find out what you are fighting against to cause that tension. You may be sure there is something there holding up your progress and preventing you from reaching your highest good. Let your only desire be to do My will and walk in My ways, and allow nothing to stand in the way to prevent it from taking place. When you take time to seek, you will know what My will is for you, and then it is up to you to obey it without hesitation. When you are working and living in harmony, you will know the meaning of true freedom, freedom of heart, mind and Spirit. You will find untold wisdom and understanding flowing from you. When you are in this state of consciousness, I can use you to help bring down the new heaven and new earth.

KNOW without a shadow of doubt that you are perfect, even as I AM perfect, and there is no blemish in you. Start right now seeing the very best in yourself, and so draw the very best out of yourself. It is there deep within you, but has become so hidden away that it is difficult to see. When you take time to realise that we are one, you will see the very best in yourself, will cease belittling yourself, and will banish all false pictures of the real self. Keep saying to yourself over and over again, 'I and my Beloved are One,' until it means something to you. When you are feeling at a very low ebb, say it quietly to yourself, and feel yourself gradually rise up out of that slough of despondency and self-pity. Keep saying it until you know the reality of those words and you see the wholeness of all life and know you are part of that life.

'B E ye transformed by the renewing of your mind.' A snake cannot grow without shedding its old skin. A baby chick cannot emerge from its shell without cracking it open. A baby cannot be born without emerging from its mother's womb. These natural processes have to come about to bring change. Step by step they take place, and nothing can stop them. If the baby chick does not have the strength to burst out of its shell, it will die. There is a right time for everything. You can try to prevent changes taking place because you feel safe and secure where you are and would rather stay in the confines of that which you know rather than move out into the unknown; but in those confines you will suffocate and die. Try to understand and accept the need to change with everything that is taking place at this time. Lift up your heart and give thanks for these changes and become part of them.

*Y*OUR work is to create the new heaven and new earth. Therefore do not dwell on the troubles and tribulations, on the disease and suffering, on the wars and strife in the world. Do not allow yourself to become involved in it, for if you do, you will become part of the disease and not the cure. As you raise your consciousness, you become immunised against the trouble in the world, and you can live and work with it all about you and yet it will not be able to touch or affect you in any way. A doctor or nurse has to be immunised to be able to work freely with highly infectious diseases, and there must be no fear in them. Let there be no fear in you as you watch the situation in the world become worse. Never despair. Simply hold on in faith, let your mind be stayed on Me, and know that all is very, very well.

A S you move forward into the new, be consciously aware of Me and of My divine presence at all times, and keep your mind stayed on Me. It will help you to keep in a raised state of consciousness so that you can move forward without any difficulty. Bring Me into everything you do, say and think. Share your all with Me. When you have nothing to hide, you know the true freedom of the Spirit. I need you free so My wonders can unfold before you without anything in you to stop them. There is much waiting to unfold; it has only just begun. Imagine the wonders and beauties, undreamed of as yet, that are waiting to reveal themselves! It will be like stepping into a new world with new ways, new laws, new ideas. Keep your sights raised. Keep the vision of the New Age ever before you. You will find yourself moving into it very naturally, and it will become a part of you.

ET there be no feeling of competition within you. When you realise everyone has a specific part to offer to the whole, all that spirit of competition will disappear and you will be able to relax and be yourself. How much simpler life becomes when you cease trying to be something you are not. You have your part to play in the whole, so play it to the very best of your ability. I tell you to love one another. Are you doing it, or are you just being tolerant, making excuses for yourself by saying that there are certain souls you cannot be expected to blend with, since you are poles apart? You are all My beloveds, and the sooner you realise it the better, for you are all one in My sight, and My love flows to each one alike. When you can accept your oneness with Me, you will be able to accept your oneness with each other.

*Y*OU do not have all knowledge and all wisdom without it unfolding gradually from within. Life is a constant unfoldment. When you were a child, you had to learn certain fundamental lessons. When you put your hand out to touch the fire, you were told that it was hot and would burn you. But if you failed to obey and went your own way and touched the fire, you were burnt and found it very painful. However, it taught you not to touch it again. In this spiritual life, you have to learn certain fundamental lessons, and if they are not adhered to, you have to take the consequences. Some people learn at great speed and are ready to move on to greater lessons, until eventually they find they are so in tune, they no longer have to learn lessons, but flow with life in perfect harmony and oneness with everything. It is the ultimate state of consciousness to be reached by everyone.

IS your heart in what you are doing? You cannot create the new heaven and new earth if what you do lacks the hallmarks of love and dedication. See that what you are doing, no matter what it is, is being done to My honour and glory. Then you will want to do it perfectly. Remember, never do a job because it has to be done. If such is your attitude, before you even start doing it, go away by yourself, seek grace, and get into tune. When your attitude has changed and you feel at peace and in harmony, then go ahead and do it. You will find when your attitude is right, you will not only be able to do it perfectly, but you will also be able to do it at greater speed. The more souls who can do what has to be done in the right spirit, the quicker will My heaven be brought down on earth.

BE like an open book, hiding nothing, with every page there for all to read. When you have nothing to hide, you know what it is like to be completely free and unfettered. Share what is in your heart and have no fear of being ridiculed. Keep very aware of Me and of My divine presence, and be as simple as a small child. Simplicity is the hallmark of this spiritual life; there is nothing complicated about it. If you feel it is complicated, it is of your own making; therefore change your attitude toward it and see what happens. Waste no more time chasing rainbows. All you need is deep within you waiting to unfold and reveal itself. All you have to do is to be still and take time to seek for what is within, and you will surely find it. The answer is there. Be very patient, wait upon Me, and all will be revealed to you at the right time.

WHAT you think, what you do, and how you behave can have a tremendous effect on the state of the world. Therefore start right now looking on the bright side of life, looking for the very best in every situation that arises. If you look deeply enough, you will find it; it is there, but sometimes it is so hidden that it appears to be lost. Know that all things work together for good for those souls who truly love Me and put Me first in everything. Your faith must be strong and unshakable. You must be willing to hold on, no matter how dark or gloomy the situation appears to be. It may even be necessary to see it get worse before it gets better. Simply know that all will work out in true perfection at the right time and that all is in My hands. Realise that I AM everywhere and in everything, that there is nowhere where I AM not, and that the ultimate goal is perfection.

SPRING is here. The New Age is here. Awake from your slumbers and behold the wonder of the times, for these are truly wonderful times you are living in. See the very best in all that is taking place. Expect changes and go along with them, allowing nothing in you to hold them up. Never be afraid of the new, of the unknown, but step out fearlessly into it, knowing that I AM with you always, and that I will never leave you or forsake you. Recognise Me in everything, and give Me the honour and glory. Know that it is the Golden Age that you are moving into, so be not concerned nor struggle against the changes which are taking place at this time. The darkest hour comes before the glorious dawn. The dawn is here; it comes in perfect rhythm, and nothing can stop it coming about. The whole of the universe functions in that perfect rhythm, so why don't you?

WHEN you long to do the right thing and take the right path, you will do so. You must be strong to be able to withstand the temptations which may beset your way and to recognise them for what they are. Every temptation overcome gives you a deeper inner strength and stability, making you able to face anything without wavering. My ways are very strange, but remember that I see the whole of the picture, whereas you only see such a small portion of it. I see all the actors in the play of life; you only see the ones nearest at hand. One by one I point the way to them, and they follow it and take their part in the whole vast overall plan; and so the plan unfolds in true perfection. Watch it unfold, and glory in the wonder of it. Accept it all with a full and grateful heart, and see My hand in all that is taking place.

WHY not start right now thinking abundance? Realise that there is no virtue in being poor. I want you to understand that money as such is neither good nor bad; it just is. It is there to be used, and it has to be kept circulating and not hoarded. It is power, and power has to be handled wisely. Electricity is power, and you do not handle that foolishly, for if you did, it would destroy you. So why handle money in an irresponsible manner? When you can accept the true freedom of the Spirit, you can shake off all sense of limitations, all sense of lack. Learn to use all you have with real wisdom, understanding that all I bestow upon you must be used to My honour and glory and that you must be a good steward of all My good and perfect gifts.

DO not attempt to look too far ahead or make plans too far ahead because if you do, they may all have to be changed. It would be best to allow everything to unfold, and you will find it will happen at far greater speed than you can imagine. Let there be no impatience about it; simply wait upon Me and see everything open up in the most marvellous way. But the timing has to be right. When winter closes in, you always feel it will never end, but before you realise what is happening, spring almost unobtrusively starts to break through. This process is what is happening with the new. Like the spring, it is here, and the winter, the old, has passed away. But you may not have fully realised or accepted it, and until you do so, your eyes will not be opened to the wonder of it all. Open your eyes and miss nothing that is taking place at this time.

A S more and more love is released into the world, a wonderful healing is taking place. It is like balm poured into wounds, healing and making whole. Love starts within the individual. It starts in you, and it grows like a seed, bursting forth revealing great beauty and wholeness. It is what is taking place now. Many souls feel that something is happening to them, but they are bewildered and do not realise what it is. They search without, hoping to find a clue which will show them what is taking place. Other souls feel a stirring but are afraid of what they feel, for it is new, it is strange and unknown, and they try to shut it out. Nothing will be able to stop this release of love. It is like the genie in the bottle; having been released, it cannot be put back again. It cannot be hidden or ignored. Gradually it will begin to reveal itself in everyone. It has come to stay.

HERE is always another rung of the ladder to be climbed. Be not faint-hearted, but go forward and upward always reaching for the highest. Life is movement; it is change; it is growth. No soul can remain in the same state all the time. Nature cannot remain static; it is ever changing and expanding, growing from one stage to the next. The acorn grows to a mighty oak; the bulb grows and produces beautiful flowers; the seed of corn produces grain. Change is taking place all the time. If change is not taking place in you, you may be sure that something is wrong, and it is necessary for you to find out what it is and then do something about it. Do not resist change, but flow with it and accept it. It may not always be comfortable, but be willing to accept a little discomfort so that the glorious new can evolve in and through you, transforming you into a new being, filled with light, love and inspiration.

PEACE be unto you. To be at one with Me is to be at peace, for peace starts deep within the soul and then reflects itself without. Then when you have found inner peace and stability, you can go anywhere and withstand anything. You can even walk in the valley of the shadow of death and fear nothing, for with that inner peace comes serenity and tranquillity which nothing and no one can disturb or destroy. As you recognise and accept your true relationship with Me, and do it as simply as a child without any complications, so will your whole life be filled with joy and thanksgiving. Then no fear can enter, and you will appear to live a charmed life, and to be fully protected, for where there is no fear, there is full protection. It is fear that opens the door to danger and leaves you vulnerable. Therefore banish fear, let My peace and love infil and enfold you, and give eternal thanks.

I AM Spirit. I AM everywhere. I AM in everything. There is nowhere where I AM not. When you fully realise this fact and can accept it, you know that the kingdom of heaven is within you, and you can cease your search and turn within. Then you find within you all you are looking for. How few souls nowadays do it! They are far too busy searching everywhere for the answers except within. When you can accept that I AM within you, never again will you feel alone; never again will you have to search without for the answer to your problems. But when anything arises which needs answering, you will seek that peace and stillness within, lay your questions and problems before Me, and I will give you the answers. Then you have to learn to obey and to follow out exactly what I reveal to you from within. You have to learn to live by My word and not just hear it.

KEEP life as simple as possible and enjoy to the full the simple wonders and beauties which are there for all to share but which are so often taken for granted. Be like a child, able to see and enjoy those little seemingly insignificant wonders in life: the beauty of a flower, the song of a bird, the glory of the sunrise, the rain drops trickling down a window pane. How simple and yet how truly beautiful they are when you look at them with eyes that really see and cease to rush through life in such a hurry that you fail to notice them! Do you see My wonders and beauties all around you? Or is your mind so full of the cares and worries of the day that you are blind and deaf and bowed down, and you see nothing for you are so wrapped up in yourself? Why not try today to keep ever aware of all that is going on around you?

NOTHING is by chance. There is a perfect pattern and plan running through the whole of life, and you are part of that wholeness and therefore part of that perfect pattern and plan. When you see strange things happening in your life and wonder why they should happen to you, take time to see how it all fits in, and you will see a reason for everything. The reasons may not always be what you expected, but nevertheless be willing to accept them and to learn by them, and do not fight against them. Life should be effortless. A flower does not struggle to unfold in the rays of the sun, so why should you struggle to unfold in the rays of My limitless love? If you do, it is of your own doing, and it is not part of My perfect pattern and plan for you. Simplicity is My hallmark, so keep life simple. Keep in constant contact with Me, and watch yourself unfold in My love.

WHEN you are in tune with life you will find yourself doing everything at the right time. All you have to do to get into tune is take time to go into the silence to find your direct contact with Me. This is why those times of peace and stillness are so vitally important for you, far more important than you realise. A musical instrument, when it is out of tune, creates discord; you, when you are out of tune, do the same. A musical instrument has to be kept in tune; you, too, have to keep yourself in tune, and you cannot do it unless you take time to be still. It cannot be done when you are rushing around, any more than a musical instrument can be tuned while it is being played. It is in the silence that the notes can be heard and be readjusted. It is in the silence that you can hear My still small voice, and I can tell you what to do.

I was shown a fledgling learning to fly. Its first efforts were very feeble. But as it used its wings more and more, they became stronger until it found the freedom of flight and was able to soar to great heights and fly great distances without any effort. I heard the words:

Faith comes with practice. Live by faith until it becomes rocklike and unshakable, and find the true freedom of the Spirit.

PRING unfolds in true perfection. This is the spring of the New Age, and it too is unfolding in that same true perfection. You are part of it, and it brings you new life. With it comes a glorious feeling of complete freedom and abandonment, of bursting out of old confined ways into new spaciousness where there are no limitations. Feel yourself growing and expanding in every direction, with a sense that anything can happen at any moment. Be like a runner at the starting line, on your toes all keyed up, ready to be off at the starter's signal. There is so much going on at all levels at this time. Changes are coming and you are part of those changes, so go along with them. Be willing to change and change quickly when and where necessary. Do not hesitate or hang back. Step right into all that is taking place swiftly and surely with absolute confidence and faith.

HERE is a time and season for everything. It is a question of allowing your life to be guided by Me so that you know the right time and season with a clear inner knowing and can move swiftly following those inner promptings with absolute confidence. When you are at peace within, time means nothing; it is when you are unhappy or uncomfortable that you find time drags, and you feel that the day will never end. When you are enjoying what you are doing, time flies by and you wish that there were more hours in a day. It is important that you learn to enjoy to the full everything you undertake and that your attitude towards it is right. You will get far more done; and it will be done with love, and therefore will be done perfectly. Let perfection be your aim at all times. When you do something with love, you are doing it for Me.

HE key to your happiness and contentment lies deep within you, within your own heart and mind. The way you start each day is very important; you can start off on the right foot or the wrong one. You can wake up with a song of joy and gratitude in your heart for the new day, for being alive, for the very wonder of living, and for being in tune and harmony with the rhythm of all life. You can expect the very best from the coming day, and therefore draw it to you. Or you can start the day with a chip on your shoulder, disgruntled and out of rhythm. You are responsible for what today will bring, and knowing it gives you an even greater responsibility than those souls who are not aware of it and therefore know no better. You cannot blame your state of mind on anyone else. It all rests with you.

WHERE are you on the ladder of life? Have you reached rock-bottom and are on the upward climb? Have you been willing to give up everything in your life to put Me first, not because you are afraid, but because of your deep love for Me and your longing to do My will and walk in My ways? Can you say, 'Let Thy will be done,' and mean it, and be willing to do whatever I ask you to do, no matter how strange or foolish it may appear to be in the eyes of others? It takes courage and such deep inner knowing and certainty that nothing will be able to throw you off balance. Only those souls who are strong will be able to follow this spiritual path. It is not for those souls who choose to go their own way and refuse to listen to My word. There are no short-cuts in this spiritual life. You have to seek and find your own salvation.

WHEN a small child starts to walk, it takes a few faltering steps until it gains confidence, and as it does so, its steps become firmer and surer until eventually it can walk without stumbling. Then it learns to run and jump, but one stage has to be reached at a time. So with faith. It has to be built up gradually; it does not come all at once. As you put your faith to the test, so will it grow until you are able to step out and live entirely by faith because your security is rooted and grounded in Me. You know you can do all things with Me, for it is I working in and through you to bring them all about, and that of your own strength you would not be able to do them. Always recognise your source of help, strength and inspiration, and never fail to give thanks for it. Take nothing for granted, but recognise My hand in everything.

HERE are many little things in everyday living that can easily cause disunity and disharmony. Rise above them and unite on what matters in life: on your love for Me, on your love for each other, on living and working for the good of the whole, and on forgetting the self and all those petty little incidents that keep rearing their heads regarding personal likes and dislikes. It is when a soul feels strongly that its way is right and flatly refuses to give one way or the other that sooner or later something has to give. When you stretch a piece of elastic until it can stretch no more, it will either break or, if released suddenly, snap back and hurt you. But if you can release it gently, it will go back into place without breaking or causing any unnecessary pain or suffering. Why not open your heart and ease that strain and tension gently? Love and understanding will always help to smooth the way.

ONLY as you expand your consciousness are you open and receptive to the new all around you and can become attuned to new thoughts, new ideas and new ways of life. Be prepared to see beyond the immediate into higher dimensions, higher realms, and open to the ways of the Spirit. There is much you can understand and accept intuitively but at which the mind boggles, so why waste time trying to work everything out with the mind? Why not be willing to live and act intuitively and inspirationally? When you do, you are functioning from a raised state of consciousness and are receptive to the new. You become a clear channel for the new to unfold in and through you. So raise your consciousness from the negative to the positive, from the destructive to the constructive, from the darkness to the light, and from the old into the new, and see what happens. You will find the old will fall away, revealing the glorious new.

EAN not on anyone. You need no outer props and reassurances, for you have all deep within you. It is inner peace that everyone longs for, and it is there when you take time to look for it. Do you take time to see the truth, or do you accept everything you hear, see and read at face value? When you know something from within, nothing or no one from without can shake it. It is something that is so real to you, it would not matter if the whole world went against you, telling you that you were wrong. You would be able to go quietly along your way without being disturbed or thrown off balance. That is the joy and strength of inner knowing. It is what can give you the peace which passes all understanding. So whenever you are in any doubt about anything, go within and seek the truth, and I will reveal it to you; then go your way in peace and confidence.

*Y*OU cannot build a mighty temple without solid foundations. You cannot build the new heaven and new earth without love, love for one another and love for Me. Love starts in the little things in life and spreads out from there. Sow seeds of love wherever you go, and see them grow and flower and flourish. Seeds of love sown in even the hardest of hearts will start to grow in the end; it may take time for the seeds to germinate, but as they are tended with loving care, they cannot fail to grow. So despair of no one; simply pour forth love unceasingly and harden not your heart. Cease trying to justify yourself or your actions. Cease blaming the other person. Search your own heart, sort yourself out, and find perfect peace of heart and mind. Then you can move anywhere in true freedom and joy, radiating love and more love. There can never be too much love. Let it flow freely.

IFE is what you make it. Why not find the very best in every situation and enjoy it to the full, no matter where you are or what you are doing? Never waste time · and energy wishing you were somewhere else, doing something else. You may not always understand why you find yourself where you are, but you may be sure there is a very good reason and that there is a lesson to be learnt. Do not fight against it, but find out what that lesson is and learn it quickly so that you can move on. You would not want to remain static, would you? As you cease resisting and simply accept the lessons to be learnt, taking them all in your stride, you will find life much easier and, what is more, you will enjoy the changes which take place. A plant does not resist growth or change; it simply flows with it and unfolds in true perfection. Why don't you do the same?

YOU are in the world but are not of it. There is no need to allow the ways of the world to drag you down. Enjoy them, but do not try to possess them or allow them to possess you. In the New Age it is not necessary to wear sackcloth and ashes or to go around declaring that you are a miserable sinner and are not worthy to be called My beloved child. All this teaching is of the old age and is false and unreal. Accept that we are one and that I AM within you. Feel yourself being lifted out of the darkness of all this false teaching into the glorious light. Leave behind all the old and let it die a natural death. Enter the new, reborn in Spirit and in truth, and know the meaning of true freedom. I need you free, not all tied up with self and self-concern. Be like a very small child, free and joyous, and live in the ever-present now.

GIVE thanks for everything you have, for everything you receive, and for everything you are going to receive. In fact, never cease to give thanks, for it is a positive attitude towards life and the very act of giving thanks which draw the very best to you. It helps to keep your heart and mind open; it helps to keep your consciousness expanding. You will always find something to give thanks for, and as you start doing it and start counting those blessings, they will increase. You will realise how mightily blessed you are, that all I have is yours, and that My storehouses of abundance are full to overflowing and you lack nothing. Your every need is wonderfully met, and in that state of consciousness you are able to give and give and never count the cost, for it is as you give that you receive. As you give, you make room for more to return to you.

I AM your source of supply, and all that I have is yours. My infinite abundance is available to all, but your consciousness must be of abundance, with no thought of lack or shortage. Feel your consciousness expand and expand, and let it go on expanding without any limitation, for limitation causes blockages in the constant flow. With limitation comes fear, and with fear stagnation; and when something becomes stagnant, the circulation is cut off and it goes dead. Keep the circulation flowing. Let there be a constant giving and receiving on all levels, and know the meaning of infinite abundance. Know that you are one with Me, that you are one with all the wealth in the world and that nothing is taken to the self, nothing is hoarded. All is there to be used wisely. Be a good steward of all My good and perfect gifts. Seek My guidance and direction as to the right use of My infinite supply.

T is important that there is balance in
every situation at all times. You will find
when everything you undertake is done
under My guidance, there will always be
perfect balance. That is why you have to
allow life to unfold without trying to force
anything, for as you do, nothing can go
wrong and nothing can be out of timing. It
does not mean that you sit and do nothing,
expecting everything to fall into your lap.
You have to keep ever alert; you have to keep
your consciousness raised; you have to expect
the very best; you have to have faith that all is
very, very well. You have to wait upon Me in
absolute faith and confidence. You have to
know without a shadow of a doubt that I AM
your constant guide and companion. You
have to know that your ways are guided by
Me and by Me alone, so that every step you
take is firm and sure and everything you do is
done in love.

HOW easy it is to lash out at the world situation and complain about it, blaming everyone but yourself for it! It is easy to say, 'Why don't they do something about it?' What about you doing something about it? Never sit back and feel helpless and imagine that you can do nothing to help. You can help and you can start helping right now. You can start by putting your own house in order. You can smooth out all those misunderstandings and try righting those wrongs. You can expand your consciousness so that you are able to see life from a different and wider angle. You can learn to be more tolerant, to be more open, more loving, and to see both sides of the picture. You can start right now banishing all bitterness, criticism and negativity in your thinking. You will find as you do your part, you will be helping the whole. But you cannot do it on your own. Do it with My help.

WHY not do in life what you enjoy doing, as long as it does not harm another soul and brings only good to yourself and all those souls with whom you are concerned? Learn to do what you are doing at the proper time and in the proper way and without great strain or effort. Small children know how to enjoy life. Become as a very small child with no inhibitions and learn to enjoy life without any restriction, self-concern or self-consciousness. Do not always do things because you feel they must be done or you have to do them. When something is done under compulsion, all the joy and pleasure go out of it. Learn to do everything because you love doing it. Give whatever you have to give for the sheer love of giving and for the sheer love of living, and see how different life will become for you.

SEEK and find your direct link with Me, and retain that link no matter what is going on all around you. That link with Me, the Divine, is the source of all power, and it is this power which creates miracles. What are miracles but My divine laws in operation? Work with those laws and anything can happen. It is identifying yourself with the oneness of all life, with all wisdom and all power, which opens doors and enables the laws to operate within you. Why stand back and watch miracles happen in the lives of others, when they can just as well happen in yours? Miracles manifest when you attune yourself to this power and oneness and can accept that you can do all things through Me, for I strengthen you and uphold you and work in and through you. Recognise that of yourself you are nothing, but with Me you can indeed do all things, and you shall behold miracle upon miracle come about in your life.

EACE starts within. It is there within every soul, like a tiny seed waiting to germinate and grow and flourish. It has to be given the right conditions, the right environment and the right treatment before it can start. Be still and create the right conditions. Be still and give it a chance to take root. Once it is well-established, it will continue to grow; but in its tender beginnings it needs to be helped and cherished. Therefore you hold the key to world peace within yourself. Do not waste time looking at the chaos and confusion in the world, but start putting things right within yourself. Quietly go about doing My will. You do not have to talk about it, but simply to live it. Transform the chaos and confusion in your own life to peace, serenity and tranquillity; and become a useful member of society and the world you live in. Start with yourself where you know you can do something, and then work outward.

WHEN life asks you to change, see clearly what is needed and change without any resistance, knowing that every change is for the very best. Change is not always comfortable, especially for those people who have set ideas and ways. You must be willing to fling out one nice, comfortable, well-established idea after another until you are completely free and open to receive something entirely new and revolutionary. Here is where the difficulty often comes. Many people, having absorbed something new, want to cling on to it and refuse to let it go. Why not see it only as a stepping stone to greater and more wonderful revelations which are there waiting to be made when you have made room for them? You cannot fill up a full bucket; you have to empty it first. You cannot move right into the new when you are still clogged up with the old and refuse to let go. So change and change quickly, for I have need of you.

WHATEVER you undertake, do it with My blessing. Never rush madly into something without first seeking My blessing. Go into the silence and feel peace and serenity enfold you, and in that state of perfect peace ask and receive My blessing. Then go forward in absolute faith and confidence and do what has to be done. Know that I AM with you all the way, and that everything will work out perfectly. The greater the task to be accomplished, the greater your need for My blessing. Why not start off by bringing Me into every small area of your life, and gradually include Me in more and greater areas until eventually you take no step without first seeking Me and My full blessing? Be prepared to take big strides forward into seemingly impossible situations, but be not afraid, for I go before you to prepare the way. Keep your consciousness raised, keep your contact with Me, and be absolutely fearless in everything you undertake, whatever it may be.

HERE is a place for each individual in the world, but you must seek and find where your place is and where you fit in. If you are afraid to take the responsibility of bringing in the new, do not try to stop those souls who are willing to do it. Realise that those souls who have been trained and inspired to undertake this task will do so, for it is their work. Find your rightful place in the whole vast plan, and if you are not in the front line do not let it disturb you. Remember, all sorts of people are needed to make up the whole. Simply accept your specific work and do what you know you have to do whole-heartedly, and allow those souls who have been placed in the position of leadership and responsibility to go ahead. Give them your full backing and complete loyalty; they need it and appreciate it. Lift up your heart in deep love, praise and gratitude for them, and always give of your very best.

OW often have you heard the remark, 'How time flies!'? When you are full of joy and happiness, giving of your very best, living for others, with the good of the whole in your heart, time does indeed fly and you enjoy every second of it. Even though you are living in time, it is not necessary to allow it to become a burden to you and drag you down. There is time for everything, for all those things you want to do, because you will make time to do them. Everyone has an equal amount of time, but it is how you use it that matters, so never complain that some souls have more time than others. Never be a slave to time, but make it your servant. You have to make up your mind what you want to do and then go ahead and do it; and you will find that you have the time to do it perfectly.

DRAW nigh to Me and I will draw nigh to thee. It is up to you to take the first step in the right direction by making your direct contact with Me, and the rest will unfold. Each soul will have a different approach, but all that matters is that you make it, no matter how faltering at first. Simply know that once you have taken that initial step, every following one will become stronger and surer. You will behold wonder upon wonder take place as you do My will and see My laws manifest in form. Your faith and belief will become strong and unshakable as you expect the very best to come about and draw it to you. See it take place, not just once but time and time again, until you can no longer doubt the wonder of My ways, until you put your entire faith and trust in Me and allow Me to take over and guide your whole life.

DO you feel that you cannot love certain people? First stop hating them. Stop being intolerant towards them and criticising them. That can be your first step in the right direction. Then gradually take time to know them, to find out what makes them tick, and to find out what it is in you that has created this separation between you and them. Look within yourself and find out what has gone wrong with you and your relationship with them, and never at any time throw the blame onto anyone else. When you can face up to yourself and your own shortcomings, you are on the right path heading in the right direction and will be able to find the perfect solution to your problems. Before you fully realise it, your whole attitude and relationship towards each soul will have changed. You can always do something right now, so why not do it instead of waiting for someone else to take the first step?

I HAVE to allow you to make mistake after mistake in life, but when you recognise them and seek My help, I AM always there to help you and show you the way. But I will not do your work for you. You must learn to do it for yourself. This life is not for weaklings, but for those souls who are strong and sure of themselves, and for those souls who want to find the answers and are willing to go all out to find the right answers, no matter what the cost. Are you afraid of making mistakes? Are you afraid of going out of your depth? You will never learn to swim unless you take your feet off the bottom. You will never grow spiritually unless you stand on your own feet. Be afraid of nothing, but in absolute faith and confidence go ahead and do what you know is right and ignore all opposition. Be guided by that inner knowing which comes from Me.

WHY not make this day a glorious day by starting off on the right foot and getting into contact with Me the instant you wake up? Why not fill your heart with love and gratitude for a day filled with expectations of the very best and highest? When your first few moments of the new day are joyous and uplifting, you will find the next few will also be so, and as the moments grow into hours, you will find that joy and peace will follow you throughout the day. When you wake up with a heavy burden on your mind, feeling low and depressed, you can carry that state of mind throughout the day unless you do something about it. Seek Me to find the perfect peace of heart and mind which comes when you have cast all your cares and worries upon Me, and when your only desire is to do My will and walk in My ways.

WHY not be an optimist in this life, always expecting the best, always finding the best, always creating the best? Optimism leads to power; pessimism leads to weakness and defeat. Let the power of the Spirit shine in and through you, creating around you a world of beauty, peace and harmony. When your outlook on life is optimistic, you lift all those souls around you, giving them hope, faith and belief in life. You will always find that like attracts like, that your optimism will create optimism and will snowball. There is always hope in life, even if it is but a tiny flickering spark to begin with. When it is surrounded with hope and love in the right atmosphere, that tiny spark will be fanned into a flame; and it will grow and grow until you are on fire with the fuel of the Spirit which is unquenchable and inextinguishable. Once it has been ignited, nothing will be able to stop it spreading.

T is not easy to turn the other cheek when someone hits out at you, in either word or deed. The immediate reaction is to hit back, but here is where reactions have to be watched with the greatest care and where self-control and complete selflessness have to be put into practice. Those souls who have not learnt self-discipline will give back as good as they get and feel justified in doing so. Then they will wonder why there is so much chaos and confusion in the world. They are so blind they cannot see that until they have learnt to change their whole outlook and start to love their neighbour as themselves, they cannot hope to change what is going on in the world. The more love and goodwill there is, the quicker will change come. But it all starts in you. Therefore the sooner you realise it, the sooner will changes take place all around you, and so out into the world. Why not start doing something about it now?

OPEN yourself to the inflow of My divine love and light. Open up the doors of your heart and allow nothing to stop that flow. Keep those doors wide open so that love and light can flow freely in and through you, and the life force is ever in evidence within you. When the doors of your heart are closed and the flow of love and light ceases, your whole life becomes stagnant, and nothing lives in a stagnant pool. That is why you have consciously to keep those doors wide open and draw from Me, the source of all life, all the time so that your heart never at any time becomes dried up and stagnant. A stream that ceases to draw its supply from its source dries up. You, when you cease to draw your supply from Me, will soon dry up and become useless. So keep consciously aware of Me, and constantly draw your life force from Me. You make your choice day by day, hour by hour, minute by minute.

*T*HE joy of giving is tremendous. As you learn to give and give whole-heartedly of the gifts and talents which are yours (everyone has different ones, and they all function on different levels), so will you grow in grace and stature. If you have a happy, sunny nature, and you give of it wherever you go, it will be returned to you a thousand-fold, for everyone responds to a sunny disposition. Always remember, 'As you sow, so shall you reap.' If you sow criticism, intolerance, disloyalty and negativity, you will reap these qualities, for you draw them to you. Why not start right now sowing seeds of joy, happiness, love, tenderness and understanding, and see what it will do to you? Your whole outlook on life will change, and you will find that you will draw the very best in life to you. The joy you give will be reflected by all those souls around you, for everyone loves a joyous giver and responds to that giving.

I was shown a mountain whose summit seemed to be cloaked in a cloud. I saw many souls moving up the mountainside and I noticed that when they reached the cloud, they hesitated and seemed afraid to move through it. I heard the words:

Fear not. Move through the cloud of unknowing into the glorious sunshine and be consciously aware of Me and My divine presence, for I AM everywhere. There is no place where I AM not.

BIG doors swing on small hinges. Tremendous happenings start from very small beginnings. I tell you, what has started at Findhorn in such a small way will grow and expand into a world-wide, universal movement; a revelation will become a revolution. My ways are very strange and very wonderful; they are not your ways. Walk in My ways in absolute faith and confidence, and see My wonders and glories unfold. The spring of the New Age is here, bursting forth in perfect harmony, beauty and abundance; and nothing can stop it from coming about. There is a right time and season for everything, and now is the right time and season for the birth of the New Age. So dwell not on the past, leave it all behind; and see what I have for you this new and glorious day. See My wonderful promises all come about, and give eternal thanks for everything. Hold ever before you the vision of the new heaven and new earth.

ITHOUT love in your heart, you cannot travel this spiritual path, for love is the key. Love points the way. Love is the way. It is a waste of time talking about love. Live and demonstrate it in your life. Forget the self completely by pouring out love to your fellow human beings. The more you love them, the more you love Me. Toleration is not enough; genuine love is what is necessary. Love is never possessive. Love sets free the loved ones. You can never hope to help a soul when you are possessive, for all souls must be completely free to find themselves and live their own lives, directed by Me. When you are possessive of a soul, you hold up that soul's spiritual progress, and it is something you must never do, for it is a very heavy responsibility you take on if you do so. Freedom of the Spirit is essential for each and every one.

WHEN your attitude is positive, you can see beyond the immediate into the very depths. See your needs very clearly, and then know without a doubt that those needs will all be wonderfully met, and give thanks that they are being met. Never fail to give thanks. The law of gratitude for everything is a fundamental spiritual law. Can you be truly grateful for everything? Can you see good in every situation? I want you to try putting this law into practice more and more, especially when you are faced with a seemingly very difficult situation. Look at it fairly and squarely; then look through it, under it, over it and all around it; and when you have finished, you will find that your whole outlook towards that situation will have changed completely. What first appeared to be a disaster has now become an opportunity, and you will be determined to make it a success by drawing the very best out of it.

BE at perfect peace. Do not strain to understand that which is not for your understanding. When I wish to convey something to you, it will be done without effort, for I will throw the light of truth onto it. It will be revealed to you, and you will be left in no doubt as to the meaning of it. When I say that life is effortless, that is exactly what I mean. There is far too much strain and effort in life. How can you hope to be at peace when you are straining and striving all the time? Let My peace which passes all understanding infil and enfold you, for when you are at peace within, you reflect peace without, and all those souls you meet will feel that peace. Let nothing disturb or distress you. Simply know that all is in My hands, and all is very, very well. So lift up your heart in deep love, praise and gratitude, and go forth this day at peace.

LOOK at the abundance of nature, of the beauty all around you, and recognise Me in everything. How many times during the day as you walk to and fro do you look at the wonders all around you and give thanks for everything? Much of the time you are in such a hurry you miss a great deal and fail to absorb these wonders and beauties which would lift and refresh your very soul. It is a question of opening your eyes and being sensitive and aware. Start right now becoming more and more aware of the things that matter in life, the things that gladden the heart, refresh the Spirit and lift the consciousness. The more beauty you absorb, the more beauty you can reflect. The more love you absorb, the more love you have to give. The world needs more and more love, beauty, harmony and understanding, and you are the one to give it forth. Why not open your heart now and do it?

BE not satisfied with yourself when your life is in turmoil, but seek for guidance and direction from within, and be willing to accept help from without. There are many times when I have to use My channels to help to throw light on a situation, especially when there are blind spots or when you are too close to a situation to be able to view it clearly yourself. At those times be willing to accept help from without, though it does not mean you have to rush to someone else every time you need a problem solved. It is important for you to learn to stand on your own feet and do your own thinking and seeking within whenever possible. You must not be spiritually lazy, relying on someone else for something you know you should be working out yourself. It takes time and patience to be still and go within to find the answer, but you cannot hope to grow spiritually unless you learn to put it into practice.

KEEP that centre within you as still as a millpond, so that you can reflect all the very best without any distortions, and then you will be able to radiate that very best outward. Allow nothing to distress or disturb you; simply know that all is working out perfectly, and take it all in your stride without a worry in the world. Learn to laugh at yourself, especially when you find yourself becoming too serious and weighed down by the ways of the world. When you find yourself becoming too serious, let go, relax and begin to enjoy life, and you will find all strain and tension will vanish. If you see yourself weighed down from carrying too heavy a burden on your shoulders, immediately release that burden and rest and relax. You will find you will be able to do far more in that state of rest and relaxation than when you are as taut as a piece of elastic, fully stretched and ready to snap.

*T*HIS spiritual life calls for souls who are completely dedicated, for without dedication you will faint along the way. There are many influences in life which can easily throw you off balance unless you are one-pointed and completely dedicated. To live a full and glorious life means living it all the time; it cannot be part-time. You have to keep on your toes day and night, to be on the alert and to act at a moment's notice without any thought of the self or self-concern. There are times when you will have to go ahead in complete faith and confidence without even knowing the reason why you are doing it. You will have to act from intuition and inspiration, and when you do there may not appear to be any rhyme or reason for it. But when you know something is right, go ahead and do it, and know you will have all the forces of light behind you, for I AM with you.

FLOW with the tide, not against it. When you feel that change is necessary, be willing to change and do not try to resist it. Be very flexible. Keep open, and never let your attitude be 'What was good enough for my parents is good enough for me.' Change will never come if that is your attitude, and changes must come. The new cannot fit into the old mould because the new has outgrown the old and needs more room. Give it more room by expanding with it. It need not be a painful process when there is no resistance. When a plant is pot-bound, it needs to be repotted to allow its roots to expand. When your consciousness has outgrown the old conceptions, it needs to be allowed to expand into new realms. This process can come about very naturally; there need not be any stress or strain. Simply let go, relax and feel yourself changing and expanding as naturally as breathing, moving out of the old into the new.

NEVER fail to give thanks for every lesson you learn, no matter how difficult it may be. Realise that only the very best is bound to come out of it, and that every difficulty is but a stepping stone along the way. There are important lessons which have to be learnt, and the sooner you learn them, the better. Never try to shirk them or get around them, but see them for what they are and face them fairly and squarely. Never be like a gramophone needle that is stuck in a groove, repeating the same old mistakes over and over again. When you want to change, you can do it. When you want to be different and live a victorious life, you simply have to make up your mind that you are going to do it, and you will do it. Why not start right now seeing the very best in life, and enjoy life as it should be enjoyed?

I AM the Source of all things. I AM the Source of your abundant supply. Think abundance; think prosperity. Never for one second think lack or poverty. When you think limitation, you create limitation; you draw it to you. Before you know it, you will find that you have dammed up the free flow of My limitless supply of all things. Next time you find yourself suffering lack of any sort, do not blame your circumstances, your conditions or your situation, but take time to look within and see what there is in you which is causing the blockage. Is it fear of lack, fear of being short of something? Fear can cause a blockage quicker than anything else. Cast all your fears and worries upon Me and let Me sustain you. Let Me infil you with power and strength, with faith and belief. Once you have your spiritual values right, you will find that the rest of your life will fall into place in true perfection.

YOU cannot know Me and walk in My ways and do My will if you do not love Me; and you cannot love Me unless you love one another. Many souls talk about their love for Me, and yet they do not know what it means to love themselves and to love their fellow human beings. The key is always love, and the most important lesson to learn is to love. You have to learn to love what you are doing, to love those souls you are with, to love your surroundings, to love where you live, to love the very air you breathe, the very ground you walk upon. Love everything you set your eyes upon. Liking something is not enough; you have to love it and love it whole-heartedly. It is good every now and again to take stock of yourself and see how much love there is in you. Take your everyday living and see how much love you are putting into everything you do, say and think.

CEASE modelling yourself on anyone else and take time to seek within to find how I have need of you and how you fit perfectly into the whole picture. Never be like a square peg in a round hole, or out of tune and out of rhythm. When you can be yourself, all stress and strain disappear because you are no longer trying to be something you are not. In fact you are no longer trying; you just are. Therefore you are at perfect peace within, and it is reflected without. Peace, tranquillity and serenity emanate from you. You create the right atmosphere wherever you go. You are a blessing, a help and an uplift to all those souls who cross your path, and you create peace and harmony in the world around you. Now let my peace and love infil and enfold you. Lift up your heart and give eternal thanks that I AM revealing the way to you.

A S you search diligently, you will surely find what you are looking for, your at-one-ment with Me, the Source of all life. But you have to take time to search. It is something that will not drop into your lap without the deep desire in you to know Me, to know the truth, and to seek until you find what it means to you. This deep spiritual experience of inner knowing only comes to those souls who want to know; therefore never dabble vaguely in these spiritual experiences. It is up to you to go forth and experience it within. How completely empty and futile life is until you start living it to the full and putting everything to the test to see whether this spiritual life is practical and worth living! Start now doing something about it. Let there be no armchair spirituality. Let it be living and vibrating and there for all to see. Let Me see you start living a life now.

HAVE faith in yourself and in your ability to do all things with My help. Then everything you undertake in life will be completed in true perfection and with real joy. Life is to be enjoyed, so why go through it dragging one foot after another as if you were carrying a heavy burden and were being weighed down by it? You may have heavy responsibilities, but there is no need to be bowed down by them. When your attitude towards them is positive, you can enjoy those responsibilities whole-heartedly, with the knowledge that you do not have to carry them alone. For I AM here and you can share all things with Me. You are never alone. The sooner you realise it and accept it as fact, the sooner will your whole attitude change to everything you undertake, and the sooner will you be able to adjust yourself to the situation you are in and enjoy everything that you are doing.

ET the words of your mouth and the meditations of your heart be acceptable to Me at all times. It is better to be still and say nothing than to open your mouth and allow unguided words to pass your lips which you may regret as soon as they are spoken. To be outspoken may cause unnecessary pain and suffering; therefore learn to control your tongue, and count up to ten before you open your mouth. It takes a mere fleeting second to say something hurtful, but it takes a long time to heal that hurt. When you learn to do everything to Me and to My honour and glory, you will not go wrong. If you will only take time and be very patient, you will see the divine spark deep within everyone. Then you will be able to fan that spark and never try to extinguish it by your criticism, intolerance and lack of understanding. You will know that all souls are equal in My sight.

ALL things are part of the whole, and you are part of that whole. When you fully realise it and can accept it, you will never again experience separation. You will never again be able to draw apart from that wholeness because it is the living, the putting into practice, that gives it life force and reality. Start right now living and putting into practice all you have been learning, and let these lessons no longer remain with you as empty words without reality. A seed does not grow until it has been put into the soil and is given the right environment. A soul does not expand and grow and find self-expression until it finds itself in the right environment, surrounded by love and understanding. In those conditions, things begin to happen, and changes come about at great speed. The old is left behind in the light of the glorious new, and growth and expansion of consciousness can take place without any restrictions.

DO unto others as you would have them do unto you. Take time to think on this law and then take action on it. As you put it into practice, you will find all selfishness and self-concern will disappear, and your love for your fellow human beings will take first place. It is when you are thinking and living for others that you find true freedom and happiness. When you are in that raised state of consciousness anything can happen, for life can flow freely without any obstructions. Refuse to see obstruction; see only opportunities. When you are wrong, set yourself right, and learn from everything. There is an answer to every problem; seek until you have found it. You need never search in vain, for as you seek diligently for every answer, you will surely find it. But remember, never expect everything to fall into your lap without playing your part and doing what you know must be done. I help those souls who help themselves.

*L*EAVE yesterday behind and waste no more time dwelling on the faults and failures which may have marred the day; they are finished and done with. Give thanks for a new day, for a day unmarred by anything. It is pure and glorious now, and it is up to you to keep it so. It is up to you to advance steadily into it in absolute confidence and faith that it is going to be a wonderful day. Everything is going to fall into place perfectly; everything is going to run smoothly. Everyone you meet will be a joy and delight to talk to, and not one negative or unpleasant thought or idea will enter your consciousness. In the newness of the day, all is very, very well. All is perfect, and you are going to keep it so with My constant help and guidance, by being consciously aware of Me and of My divine presence, and by waiting upon Me in quietness and confidence.

HERE I AM, there is freedom, there is liberty. Where I AM, there is fullness of life, there is joy unspeakable. All souls can find this state of consciousness if only they would take time to be still and to seek within. I AM within you, so cease seeking without. Cease chasing the end of the rainbow, and find that which you are looking for deep within you. What good does it do you knowing all these facts in theory? Why not cease dealing in theory and get down to putting all you know into practice? Why not start right now and become consciously aware of Me and of My divine presence? Why not invite Me to share your all with you and take time to walk and talk with Me and to listen to My still small voice? Come closer, ever closer. Feel that oneness, the wonder of being at perfect peace deep within because you are aware of your oneness with Me.

EVER try to interfere with anyone else's path. All souls have to find their own path and reach the goal their own way. Some may do it through meditation, some through contemplation, some through prayer, some through work, and some through contact with people. Let all souls find their own path and follow it. Let there be no turning down cul-de-sacs, no wandering off down highways and byways, wasting precious time and energy. Follow the straight and narrow path. Keep your eye on the goal which is your realisation of oneness with Me, the Lord your God, the divinity within you. Never be put off when the going is hard and rough, but keep on and know you will get there. This life is not for those souls who are faint-hearted and who are afraid to face the truth and walk straight into the light. Be strong and of good courage. Put your hand in Mine, and I will guide you every step of the way, if you will only let Me.

NLESS you allow a very small child to do things for itself, to feed itself, to walk, to dress itself, to write, to draw, to express itself, it will never develop and become independent and be able to stand on its own feet and make its own decisions. You have to stand back and allow it to make mistakes and to take a long time to master what it is learning to do. You have to be very patient and wait and watch, no matter how tempted you are to do it for the child to save time. Open your eyes and realise that life is a classroom in a school, and you are learning all the time. How often do I have to stand back and very lovingly watch you fumbling and struggling with life so that you can learn a vitally important lesson, a lesson never to be forgotten once it has been learnt and mastered? I have infinite love and patience.

WHATEVER you do, do it with love; do it to My honour and glory; and never be concerned about it. When you do everything with the right attitude, it is bound to be done perfectly, so take this right attitude into everything you do. Keep ever before you the saying 'Work is love made visible'; then you will work with joy and contentment, and work will never be a chore or something that has to be done. What a difference the right attitude to work will make to yourself and to all those souls around you! If you want to succeed in what you are doing, learn to love it and handle it the right way, with that right attitude. Often it is a question of changing your attitude from negative to positive which can uplift the most mundane job. Every soul feels in harmony with a different job. What do you feel in harmony with? Is there something you love doing? Then do it!

OVE out of your little puddle and expand your consciousness, realising that there is no limitation. Many people can see no further than themselves or the group or community that they are living in. They get so tied up by small, petty things that they have difficulty in expanding in any way. Here is where tremendous changes have to come and come quickly. Do not be satisfied to accept just what you can understand, but be willing to go further and to step right out of your depth and do the seemingly impossible. In this way your capacity is stretched. Let it be stretched until you feel it is going to snap, and then let it stretch even further. Live on the brink of something completely new. Be not afraid of the new and the unknown, but simply take one step at a time in absolute faith and confidence, knowing that every step will lead you to the wonderful new heaven and new earth.

CAN you truthfully say you love your fellow human beings, that you are interested in them, that you appreciate them and know them as your family? Or do you just tolerate them and find it a real effort to have to rub shoulders with them? You cannot say you love Me if you do not love your fellow human beings, for relationships are so closely interwoven that it is impossible to love one without the other. Do you spend time picking and choosing whom you are going to love and whom you feel you could not possibly love? There should be no discrimination in love, for divine love embraces all alike. It sees all people in My image and likeness, no matter what colour, race, sex, creed or religion. You will have to reach the point when you can see and understand the oneness of all life, know the true meaning of the family of all human beings, and know Me as the source of all.

RING down My heaven upon the earth. It is up to you to do it by the way you live and by your attitudes towards life. Life is wonderful, but you have to open your eyes and see the wonder and glory of it. You must be willing to see all the good in life and to concentrate on it, ignoring the bad, the negative and the destructive and giving them no life force. All around you are the wonders and beauty of nature, and yet you can go through a whole day without even noticing what is around you. What a lot you miss in life by simply shutting it out of your consciousness and by refusing to raise your consciousness to the state where you blend with all life! Take time to stop, look and listen, so that you miss nothing and can enjoy everything. Then give eternal thanks for it all. Start this day to create a better world around you.

EVERY soul needs to withdraw from the world from time to time to find that peace which passes understanding. Every soul needs to be stabilised, and it can come about only in peace and stillness. Once that inner stability has been established, you can go anywhere and do anything without the outer chaos and confusion affecting you in any way. It is going into the secret place of the Most High. It is finding your oneness with Me, which enables you to go on when you feel you have come to the end of your tether and cannot go a step further. It is those steps taken into the unknown, in faith, in My strength, which work wonders and which change lives. It is those steps which enable the impossible to become possible and bring down My kingdom on earth, that glorious new heaven and new earth. Move always towards this end. Change and change quickly when change is needed. I AM with you always. Draw upon Me.

BEFORE you climbed a high mountain, surely you would test all your equipment to see that it was sound and that the rope had no flaws in it, for your very life would depend on it. You would choose a good guide and would need to have absolute confidence in that person. You would have to be willing to follow the guide's instructions and obey orders without question. So with this spiritual life. Until you have learnt discipline and obedience, until you choose to do My will and obey My voice, you cannot hope to start on this life of adventure. It would not be safe for you to do so. If you feel you are stuck in a rut, take stock of yourself and find out what it is deep within that is holding you up. What are you doing about self-discipline? Can you say 'no' to yourself yet? What about obedience? Are you willing to follow My will no matter what the cost?

YOU are the point of light within My mind. You are the point of love within My heart. When you can accept it, when you can see yourself as the microcosm of the macrocosm, you will never again belittle yourself or think ill of yourself. You will realise that you are indeed made in My image and likeness, that we are one, and that nothing and no one can separate us. If you feel any separation from Me, it is of your own making, for I never separate Myself from you. You are individually what I AM universally. Is it any wonder you have to be born again to accept the wonder of this truth? So many souls have strayed so far from Me, and have separated themselves to such an extent that they have placed Me in the heavens at such heights that I AM unapproachable. I AM within you, hidden in the very depths waiting to be recognised and drawn forth.

OU can be told about spiritual truths; but only as you live them, put them into practice in your life and demonstrate them do they become reality to you and live and move and have their being in you. You must do your own thinking, your own living and your own working things out. You must stand on your own feet and never expect anyone else to do it for you. Turn within, seek within for every answer, and you will find it. It may take time. You may need to learn to be patient and wait upon Me, but when your faith and belief are strong enough, you will find all you are seeking. Learn to stretch, to grow and expand. Learn to draw from the source of all power, all knowledge, all wisdom and all understanding. Keep turning to Me, the Lord your God, the divinity within you. I will never fail you nor forsake you, for surely you know by now that I AM with you always.

START right now to expand your consciousness and to think abundance in everything, for only in this way can all your needs be met. I want you to know that it is My good pleasure to give you the kingdom, for it is out of the kingdom that all else flows. That is why you have to seek it first; then all else shall be added unto you. I know your every need, and your every need is being wonderfully met. Believe it with all your heart. Never at any time allow a single doubt in to mar the wonder of it. Accept My word, live by it, and see miracle upon miracle take place. The time of miracles is certainly not over. As you live a life completely dedicated to Me, you shall witness wonders untold. You shall see the impossible made possible. You shall recognise My hand in everything. Your heart will overflow with love and gratitude for all that will take place.

I was shown a big heavy door which was very hard to open because the hinges were stiff. Then I watched a few drops of oil being placed on the hinges and the door being gently eased until it could be opened with just the slightest touch of a finger. I heard the words:

Use the oil of love more and more, for it is love that eases. It is love that will always find a way. Open your heart and let the love flow freely.

WHY not make a habit of approaching life in the right spirit, joyously, expectantly, and with absolute faith that only the very best is for you? I want you to have all the very best in life. I do not want you to go through life with a heavy weight on your shoulders, bowed down by the cares of the world. I need you free so that I can work in and through you. Stop being a worrier, and cast all your cares and burdens upon Me. Know that the kingdom of heaven is within you; it is there waiting for you to recognise it. You must know it, believe it, and then bring it about. The kingdom of heaven is a state of mind, and it is for everyone to seek and find. Every soul has to long for it before they can find the kingdom of heaven. The desire must be there and must be so strong that nothing will be allowed to stand in the way.

*Y*OU can do all things when your faith and trust are in Me, and you have no doubts and fears to hold you back. There is nothing you cannot do, nothing you cannot accomplish in this life, when your attitude and outlook are right and you have complete confidence in your ability to do it. You have within you all power, all wisdom, all strength, all intelligence and all understanding. It is I working in and through you who enables you to accomplish the seemingly impossible. Never be afraid to aim high; never be afraid to expect the impossible to become possible. Do not live within your limits; live way beyond yourself, and therefore give Me the opportunity to show you how all things are possible with Me. If you do not give Me the opportunity, how can you expect to know what can be accomplished when I AM in contact and AM guiding and directing your life? Let go, and let Me take over and see what happens.

WHERE are your faith and trust? You cannot live this spiritual life without faith and trust in Me. Let Me guide your every step. Seek Me constantly in the silence, and let Me reveal to you the next step to be taken; then take it fearlessly and with real joy. How can you expect to undertake the greater tasks in life and be given greater responsibilities until you have learnt to obey and carry out the simpler ones? How can you hope to take the world on your heart if you have not even learnt to love one another and learnt to work in peace and harmony with each other? A child has to learn to walk before it can run. You have to learn to love one another and to bring peace and harmony into your immediate surroundings before you will be able to bring about world harmony. Get yourself sorted out first. Then I will be able to use you to help and serve your fellow human beings.

NEVER be wholly satisfied with your outlook on life. There is always something new and exciting to learn about, and you can only hope to do it if you keep open and sensitive to all that is taking place. The very new is not always easy to understand. Do not allow it to concern you, but be willing to accept it in faith, and know that your understanding will grow as you do so. You will know by that deep inner knowing whether these new ideas, new ways and new thoughts are of the truth or not. If you get that deep feeling of rightness, allow yourself to absorb these truths even if you do not understand them fully. Gradually the light will dawn, and you will awaken to the meaning of it all. You cannot go on for the rest of your life in the same old way. You must be willing to branch out into something new.

DO you know what it means to love, to feel your heart filled with such joy and gratitude that you cannot contain it, and it has to bubble over and out to all those souls around you? It is a glorious feeling of well-being and of being at one with all life. All fear, all hatred, jealousy, envy and greed disappear when love is there, for there is no place for those negative, destructive forces in the presence of love. When your heart is cold and you feel no love, do not despair, but look around and find something you can love. It may be some very small thing, but that small spark can ignite your whole being until love is aflame in you. Only a small key can unlock a heavy door. Love is the key to every closed door. Learn to use it until all doors have been opened. Start right where you are. Open your eyes, open your heart, see a need and answer it.

EVERYTHING that takes place in your life happens because of your consciousness. Raise your consciousness and you raise your whole being, your whole outlook on life, and you start to live the full and glorious life which is your true heritage. You can be told about it, and you can see others living it; but until it enters your consciousness and you can accept that it is for you, nothing happens. The most seemingly simple and child-like soul can accept the kingdom of heaven far more easily than the most deeply intellectual soul who thinks it knows all the answers with its mind, but its consciousness has not been raised to higher levels. Every soul can reach a raised state of consciousness. But it is something to be achieved from within, from inner knowing, from inspiration and intuition which require no outer knowledge and wisdom. It is all there within every soul, simply waiting to be recognised, drawn forth and lived.

HY not excel in everything you do? To be good at anything, you have to keep on practising until you have mastered it. Why do you imagine that you can have perfect results in this spiritual life if you only dabble in it? Stop being a dabbler and plunge in whole-heartedly. This life calls for everything you have to make it work, so why not give all you have and see what happens? It does not matter what it is in life, nothing will live and become part of you until you have put it into practice and have seen how it works. Start right now getting down to the art of living this spiritual life. Keep on experimenting with it, and be not put off if you do not get immediate results. Simply go on applying the principles and eventually you will see how wonderfully it all works out. It is a truly glorious life when you are willing to give yourself completely to it.

WHAT is your first thought on waking? Is it one of pure joy for another wonderful day, or do you dread what today might bring? Is it an effort to get into tune and into rhythm with this day? Can you wake up with a song of praise and thanksgiving in your heart? What a difference it will make for you when you can do it, when you can start the day by putting on rose-tinted spectacles and seeing everything through them throughout the day. Start out on the right foot. Be not concerned about tomorrow; the only thing that matters is today, what you do today and what you make of it. Simply know that you can and will make a real success of today and that everything you do will be done perfectly. Know that everything you say will be said with love, that everything you think will be of the highest, and that nothing but the very best will be yours today.

OU are part of My infinite plan. You have a part to play in the overall picture. It may be only a very small part; nevertheless it is essential for the completion of the whole. Never at any time feel that your part is so small that it is not necessary. Who are you to judge? I need you in your rightful place playing your specific part. If you have not yet found out what your part is, it is up to you to seek and go on seeking until you have found what it is. See yourself fitting into your rightful place, giving what you have to give to the whole; and so feel part and parcel of that wonderful wholeness, no longer separate or divided. No one can do it for you. You have to do your own seeking and your own finding. No one else can live your own life for you. Only you can live it.

IFE can never be dull or mundane once you have placed your foot upon this spiritual path because it sets life in motion and nothing remains static. The new will be able to unfold all around you and within you in true freedom and perfection. Are you satisfied to go along in the same old way? You are free to do so, but do not expect anything very uplifting to happen in your life if that is your choice. You cannot expect big changes to take place; you cannot expect to be used by Me to help bring down the new heaven and new earth. Those souls who choose to go their own way must be willing to accept the consequences, but those souls who are willing to do My will and walk in My ways usher in the New Age. Why wait until tomorrow to make your choice? Choose now.

IT is in the stillness that all will be clarified. It is in the stillness that you become at peace and can find Me. I AM always here, but you are blind to this wonderful fact until you can become still and seek Me in the silence, and you can do it at all times. The more often you put it into practice, the more natural it becomes until you can do it as naturally as breathing. You do not have to rush off to be by yourself to find Me. You will be able to find Me at all times and in everything you are doing. It does not matter what chaos and confusion are all around you or what outer noise there may be. You can go into that inner peace and silence and find Me. When you have found Me, the light of truth will shine on every situation, for where I AM, there is no darkness; there are no problems. There is only peace.

HE beauty of life is everywhere around you. Open your eyes and see it, absorb it, appreciate it, reflect it and become a part of it. When you expect to see beauty, you will see it; whereas when you expect to see ugliness, you will do so. The choice is always yours. Drink deeply from the fountains of beauty and you cannot help reflecting it, for what is within is reflected without. You are like a mirror; you cannot hide that which is within you, no matter how hard you may try to do so, for that which is within cannot be contained. Sooner or later it will express itself in the outer world; therefore let it flow freely, and never try to stop that flow. Raise your consciousness and you will be able to see beauty in everything and everyone. You will see Me reflected there, for I AM beauty, harmony and perfection. Learn to express that beauty and harmony in everything you think, say and do.

OUR right attitude towards everything is so very important. You cannot grow and expand spiritually when your attitude is negative and you see only the difficulties and obstacles in life. There is good in every situation if you would only take time to look for it, just as there is always something to give thanks for. It is when you have no love in your heart that you are blind to the best in your situation, to the good in those souls around you, and to this wonderful life which is yours. How mightily blessed you are! But unless you are willing to accept it and recognise it and give thanks for it, you go around with a blindfold over your eyes bemoaning your lot in life. Take time to take stock of yourself, and if you feel completely stuck, the quickest way to change that situation is to start giving to others. Life is what you make of it. What are you making of your life?

WHY condemn yourself for your seeming inadequacies, mistakes, faults and failings? Why not, instead of dwelling on the negative in your life, turn those weaknesses into strengths and your faults and failings into virtues by allowing the positive to express itself in your life? Find deep within yourself real beauty, virtue and goodness. Have faith that it is there and you will find it when you search for it. When you refuse to see the best in yourself and choose to dwell on all the negative within you, you must be willing to accept the consequences, for you draw to you what you hold in your thoughts. As you think, so you are. Think the very best, and you will draw the very best to you. Know that you can do anything when I AM with you, leading and directing you. When you accept that I AM within you, how could it be otherwise?

YOU hold great power in your hands; see that you use it aright for the benefit of the whole. Power can be used positively or negatively; it is simply up to you how you use it. When you want only to see the very best results, and you use it positively, the most wonderful happenings can take place. When the power of electricity is used positively, it can turn huge machines; it can light up cities; it can do the most amazing things. But when it is used the wrong way, the results can be devastating. So it is with spiritual power, which is even greater. It is there waiting to be used, but it must be used the right way. Then only good can come from it, and you will behold wonder upon wonder unfold in true perfection. Those souls who are ready and prepared to use this power properly are being employed to help at this time to bring down the new heaven and new earth.

EE that you have an aim, a goal in life. Never be satisfied to drift through life like a ship without a rudder, being blown about by every wind of change; for without a definite aim, you will get nowhere. You must know where you are going and what you are doing. Far too many souls are willing to let themselves drift through life with the result that they accomplish nothing very constructive. Find inner peace and certainty, and without any stress or strain follow the path that you know is yours. Do what you know you must do because it is something which has been revealed to you from within, not from without. Always know from within that what you are doing is right; then you can go right ahead and sweep all obstacles aside with real strength and conviction. Know that I AM your compass, I AM your guide, and I will lead you to your goal, no matter how difficult the path may appear to be.

LWAYS remember that all roads lead to Me. Some of them may be more winding and tortuous than others. Some may appear to be very strange and even unnecessary to you, but let it not concern you. Simply let each soul find his or her own path and follow it, and you find yours. It matters not how different it may appear. Know that you will all reach the same goal in the end: your realisation of oneness with Me. There is the straight and narrow path which leads directly to Me, but to many souls it appears too simple and straightforward, and they cannot accept that it can possibly lead to Me. Instead they choose the more difficult and devious ones, thinking that by self-sacrifice and suffering they are gaining greater merit on the way. All this struggling is quite unnecessary, but human beings have free will and therefore are completely free to choose whichever way they wish. So live and let live, and be not critical of one another.

N the days ahead there will be many conflicting ideas and ways. You will be tested up to the hilt, and you will be thrown on your own. Do not try to clutch at every straw that passes by you. Simply seek within, draw your strength from Me, and go your way in peace. All doubts and fears will flee from you, and you will stand firm and steady as a rock in that inner knowing. It will matter not how the wind and storms may rage from without, for you will remain completely unaffected. I need you strong and of good courage, knowing the truth from within, which no one can take from you. Be not sucked into the whirlpool of conflict and distress that is in the world at this time; but find that haven of peace within and know Me, for I AM your anchor. I AM your haven. Let My peace and love infil and enfold you.

WHAT is age to you? Do you fear growing old? Or are you one who takes it all in your stride and who knows and understands that the fountain of youth is in your own consciousness? When you keep your mind young, fresh and alert, there is no such thing as growing old. When you have many interests in life and when you enjoy life to the full, how can you ever grow old? Human beings limit themselves when they think of three score years and ten as being the fullness of life. It can be just the beginning for many souls when they awake to the wonder of life, and in awakening begin to enjoy it. Banish all thoughts of old age. It is but a universal thought form which has become so strong that it is like a very hard nut, tough to crack. Start readjusting your thinking about age now.

OW vitally important is your right attitude to giving! Give quietly and confidently and, above all, do it with love and joy. Anything that is given begrudgingly carries with it the wrong vibrations, and therefore the perfect cannot come out of it. See that everything you do is done with love, even if you do not fully understand why you are doing it. The most ordinary, mundane job when done with love can bring wonderful and amazing results, so let the love flow freely with everything you undertake. Realise that what you are doing is needed and that no job or action is too small or insignificant. When all souls give of their very best, the weight and responsibility do not fall on the shoulders of the few. The burden is lightened for the whole, until it is no longer a burden but a real joy and pleasure. Watch your attitude, and contribute to the joy and smooth running of the whole.

ECAUSE yesterday was not all it should have been does not matter; yesterday is finished and gone, and you can do nothing about it. Today is a completely different matter; it lies before you, untouched and unblemished, and it is up to you to make it the most wonderful day. How do you start off each day? Remember, it is no concern of anyone else. It is something you and you alone have to choose to bring about. Try to start the day off with inner peace and contentment by taking time to be still and allowing that peace to infil and enfold you. Do not rush into the day unprepared and out of harmony. If you do, it is easy to take that state of mind into the day, allowing it to affect the whole of the day and all those souls you contact. It is up to you to choose what today is going to be and then make it so. Why not choose now?

CHANGE is the key that will open all doors for you, change of heart and mind. When your security is in Me, you will not fear changes, no matter how drastic they may appear to be. Simply know that every change which takes place is for the very best and for the good of the whole, whether they are personal changes, changes in the country, or in the world. Simply accept that these changes must come, and go along with them. Move forward and upward and accept it when I tell you that the best is yet to be. You will find the new far more wonderful than the old as you move swiftly into it without any further resistance. Why make life more difficult for yourself? That is what you are doing by resisting. Nothing can stay My hand. The ball has started to roll; the new day is here, and you are part of it if only you will accept it and go with it; otherwise you will be left behind.

HOW can you hope to grow without being stretched, without being tested? Where do your faith and security lie? From whence do you draw your strength and power? Are you trying to live this life on your own strength, relying on the self to pull you through? If you are, you will not be able to withstand the stresses and strains all around you. But when you place everything in My hands and allow Me to guide and direct you, you will be able to do anything because with Me all things are possible. Do you feel the burden you are carrying is too heavy and that you have been given far too great a task to carry out? Why not start right now to cast all your burdens and cares upon Me, and let Me navigate you through these troublesome waters? I will pilot you through every difficulty into calm and still waters, and free you from every strain when your faith and trust are wholly in Me.

DEDICATE yourself this day to Me, to My service, and to the service of humanity. Service is a wonderful healer, for as you forget yourself in service, you will find you will grow and expand in the most wonderful way. You will reach great heights and plumb great depths, and your love and understanding of life will begin to mean something to you. This day will afford you countless opportunities for stretching and growing. Accept each one with a heart filled with love and gratitude, and feel yourself growing in consciousness and in wisdom. Live it fully and abundantly with no restrictions, no limitations. Expect only the very best in everything and everyone, and see it come forth. Keep your heart open to one another. Look for the highest good in each other, and work from that higher level of consciousness. Encourage one another in every way possible; every soul needs encouragement. You will find as you help others, you help yourself to grow at the same time.

SEEK and find the freedom of the Spirit; for where there is true freedom, there is peace; and where there is peace, there is love; and it is love that unlocks all doors. Where there is love, there is no criticism, no condemnation and no judgement, for you know and understand that all is one in Me and in My love. You see the family of humanity and that all are created in My image and likeness. You go beyond the outer to the very heart of the matter, where there is no separation and all blend together in complete oneness. You see the very best in everyone and everything. When you are at perfect peace within, you no longer spend your time trying to change others. You simply learn to be, and in being you create a sense of oneness with all life, and peace and love reign supreme.

ONCE a chick has emerged from its shell or a butterfly from its chrysalis, there is no going back, but there is a continuous unfolding into the new. Let the action of unfolding be a day-by-day, hour-by-hour, minute-by-minute process for you. Feel the excitement and expectancy in all that is taking place. There is never a dull moment in this life when you keep on your toes; there is always something happening. Let it happen, and never try to hold up progress, but go along with it all. I tell you, all that unfolds will be for the very best and for the growth and benefit of the whole. Find that perfect rhythm in life and give of your very best to it. Flow with it, not against it, for only in this way will you find peace of heart and mind; and when you are at peace within, you are open and ready for the new to unfold.

BE willing to move forward fearlessly and to pioneer seemingly new ways, new concepts and new ideas. Be willing to break down old barriers and reveal the light of truth. I say 'seemingly new' because nothing is new. It is a question of moving full cycle; of once again finding your oneness with Me; of once again learning to walk and talk with Me as it was in the beginning; of being reborn in Spirit and in truth. Feel yourself growing and expanding. Feel the old drop away from you, and put on the new with joy and thanksgiving. How glorious is that new, how wonderful are My ways! Become consciously aware of Me and of My divine presence, and rejoice, for My kingdom is come. Let My peace and love infil you and enfold you. Lift up your heart in deep love, praise and gratitude, and be at perfect peace as you go forth this day and do My will and walk in My ways, glorifying Me.

WHEN a cupboard is full to overflowing and the doors are opened up, that which is within comes tumbling out and nothing can stop it. When floodgates are opened, the water rushes forth with tremendous power and force, carrying all before it. So with the spiritual power within you; once it has been recognised and released, nothing can stop the flow. It pours forth, sweeping aside all negativity and disharmony, bringing with it peace, love, harmony and understanding. It is love that will overcome the world; it is love which will unite all humanity. Therefore the sooner you release that tremendous power of love within you and allow it to flow freely, the sooner will you behold world peace and harmony and the oneness of all humanity. When you have love in your heart, you draw the very best out of everyone, for love sees only the best and therefore draws forth the best. Be not afraid; open up, hold nothing back, and let it all flow freely.

E not overburdened by all that has to be done. Simply learn to take one step at a time and know that each step leads you one step nearer the goal. Do not try to run before you can walk, or undertake something that is too much for you, so that you have to drag yourself along, with every step an effort. Doing so is not the right attitude; it is not being filled with My joy and freedom. It means you are trying to do it on your own strength; it means that you have separated yourself from Me and have lost the vision. Stop what you are doing, and then change your whole attitude. Hand it all over to Me, and then relax and enjoy what you are doing in a completely new way. Change of attitude can come in the twinkling of an eye, so change and change quickly, and dance and sing through this day hand in hand with Me.

ARE you consciously aware of Me and My divine presence? Do you wake up each day with a song of love and gratitude in your heart? Are you ready for whatever the day may bring, knowing that it will be a wonderful day because I go before you to prepare the way? Do you expect the very best to come out of this day and see everything falling into place perfectly? Can you see all the beauty and wonder in the world, or do you find yourself concentrating on the chaotic state the world is in, bemoaning the fact that humanity is the cause of it? Realise that without faith you cannot live this life, for it is by faith that all things are made possible. It is by faith that you can do all things, but of yourself you can do nothing. Let Me work in and through you so all may come to know Me and love Me and want to walk in My ways and do My will.

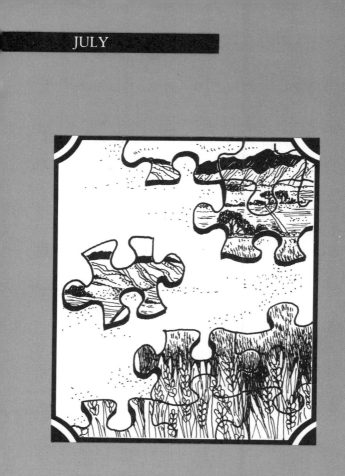

I was shown a jigsaw puzzle scattered all over a huge table. I watched as the puzzle was being put together and I saw how each piece fitted into its rightful place perfectly. I heard the words:

When you are in your rightful place
doing your own specific part,
there can be no conflict and My plan can
unfold in true perfection.

REJOICE and give eternal thanks, for you know that you live forever. You do it one day at a time, living each moment fully and gloriously, forgetting the past, with no concern for the future, simply accepting that life is eternal and has no beginning and no end. All the time you are growing and expanding in consciousness, you are beginning to understand the mystery and wonder of life eternal and your realisation of oneness with Me, the Creator of life. Step by step you move onward and upward filled with peace, tranquillity and serenity, realising that as all is in My hands, you have nothing to concern yourself with. It is when you try to look too far ahead that life becomes a real burden, and to many souls brings fear, uncertainty and even lack of faith and belief. Become as a little child, free and joyous, and life will be a continual source of delight for you. Believe in life and live it fully.

YOU cannot prove anything unless you put it to the test. You have to step out in faith and do the seemingly impossible. You have to learn to live beyond yourself, beyond your limits, to prove that with Me all things are possible. Just to live within your own small confined self, afraid to reach out beyond your limits, afraid to put life to the test, will get you nowhere, and you will fail to see My hand in everything. Fear nothing; simply know I AM with you always and will guide and direct your every step. Show the world that all things do work together for good for those souls who truly love Me and put Me first in everything. Expect miracle upon miracle and see them come about. Behold the manifestation of the new heaven and new earth as you learn to live this life and make it work. See wonder upon wonder come about because you are living and putting it all into practice.

GET into tune, find your own note, and sound it loud and clear, for you are part of the vast orchestra of life. You have your own specific part to play, so do not try to play anyone else's part. Seek and find your own and stick to it. When you learn to do it, all will be very, very well with you. It is those souls who seek to play someone else's note who will find themselves out of harmony with the whole. Never try to be like anyone else or do what someone else is doing. I do not want you all to be identical, like peas in a pod. I need you all different with your own individual gifts and qualities. An orchestra made up of all the same instruments would be very dull. The more instruments there are blended together in perfect harmony in the orchestra, the richer and more wonderful the sound which comes forth.

BLESSED are they which do hunger and thirst after righteousness, for they shall be filled.' When your longing is strong enough, it will be fulfilled, for you will search and search for the answer and will not be satisfied until you have found it. You will have the determination, patience, perseverance and persistence to leave no stone unturned until you have found what you are looking for along this spiritual path, your realisation of oneness with Me. Never be disheartened or feel you are chasing the end of a rainbow, but simply know that you will find what you are looking for in the end if you do not faint along the way or give up in despair. As every obstacle is worth overcoming to reach the goal, be determined to find the way around it, and never at any time feel anything is insurmountable or impossible. Be strong and of good courage, and go on and on and you will surely get there.

OUR thoughts towards abundance determine whether all your needs are met or not. When you think lack or poverty, and when you allow fear, worry, inferiority, greed, selfishness and anxiety into your consciousness, and when you dwell on these negative states, you draw the worst to you. When you think as a pauper, you are a pauper, for you deprive yourself of all the good things in life which are yours when you readjust your thinking and attitude towards them. Start right now thinking prosperity. See yourself with all your needs being wonderfully met. Refuse to see yourself short of anything, for if you are short of something, the shortage is in your own consciousness. Why stop the flow of My abundant, limitless supply by your limited, constrictive consciousness? When you begin to understand and to accept where everything comes from, and when you can give thanks for everything freely and joyously to Me, the giver of every good and perfect gift, you will lack nothing, absolutely nothing.

PUT your complete faith and trust in Me, and know that I will never fail nor forsake you. Nothing you undertake is impossible, for you can do all things with Me. Live by faith. I want you to see good come out of every situation no matter how seemingly strange the situation may appear to be. Be willing to have your faith and trust tested over and over again, for what is the use of talking about faith and trust if you do not put them to the test and see how they work for you? Are you willing to step out in complete faith and do the seemingly impossible, not out of bravado, but because you know without a shadow of a doubt where it comes from? Until you have tested your faith and found it unshakable, do not talk about it. Draw your strength and ability from Me, and when I AM with you, who can be against you?

*Y*OU cannot say you love Me and hate your fellow human beings, for love and hate are like oil and water: they do not mix. When you truly love Me, you will love your fellow human beings. You will love one another. You will have compassion and understanding towards one another. When you love one another, you will love Me. They are so intertwined that they cannot be separated. How great is your love for one another? Are you willing to put yourself out for another soul? Love does not have to be expressed in words; it is seen and felt in action. It radiates from you. Love is the language of silence. It can be understood and accepted without a word being spoken. It is an international language understood by the heart, not by the mind. It matters not what nationality you are, you can always convey love and communicate it in complete silence. Your eyes, your heart, your attitude, your whole being can convey what you are feeling toward another soul.

START the day aright in oneness with Me. Then nothing that happens to you during the day can throw you off balance. When you first begin to live this spiritual life, you have to make a conscious effort to get into tune, but as you live it more and more and it becomes a part of you, it is no longer an effort, and you live in such a way that it is you. You find great joy and freedom. You do not have to spend half your time in prayer seeking forgiveness, afraid of doing the wrong thing or worried in case you are off beam and are going against the stream. When you make mistakes, you accept forgiveness straight away and are determined not to make the same mistakes again. You move on, until living in this way ceases to be an effort and becomes a real joy, and you know what it is to be at one with Me and to be at perfect peace.

O get into rhythm with life you have to learn the art of being still, for the more still you become, the more clearly can you reflect the qualities of your soul. How easy it is to blame your environment, your situation or your conditions for the state you are in! It is high time you ceased doing it and realised that you have only yourself to blame. When you seek and find that inner peace and stillness, nothing and no one without will be able to disturb it or throw you off balance. Look around you; look at the beauty and perfection of nature. Everything in nature is in rhythm. There is perfect law and order in My universe. Nothing is out of tune; there is a time and reason for everything. It is there for all souls to see and to partake of, so get into tune with it. Flow with it, and be part of that law and order in My universe.

HOW vitally important is your right and positive attitude towards today and all that it holds for you! You can make or mar the day for yourself simply by the way you approach it. Your reactions to things as they take place can make all the difference. When your reactions are negative and aggressive, you immediately put up barriers and create opposition, finding fault and blaming everyone else. You are so blind you fail to see that you are the one at fault, and you go around with a chip on your shoulder. When your reactions are positive and constructive, all barriers come tumbling down and you will find you will get help and cooperation from every side. If you have made a mistake, admit it, say you are sorry and move on. Then no precious time is wasted in trying to justify yourself and prove you are right. You have many lessons to learn. Learn them quickly, and try never to make the same mistake twice.

WHAT does life mean to you? Do you enjoy it to the full? Do you expect the very best from it? Do you accept that it is infinite, that it has no beginning and no end? Does the knowledge thrill and uplift you, or does it horrify and depress you? Your attitude towards life at this time is most important, for many wonders are unfolding, and it is necessary that you go along with all that is happening and do not fight against it. It is a time of unfoldment, not of strife or struggle; therefore be still, behold wonder upon wonder unfold in true perfection, and give eternal thanks. Give thanks for being alive and for being part of what is taking place. Give thanks for the rapid changes, and change with the changes. All is for the very best; therefore be not afraid but move forward joyfully. Feel yourself a part of the whole process of change, of wholeness and of newness.

YOU are surrounded by beauty everywhere. Open your eyes and see it, and give constant thanks for it. Let the things of beauty transform you and inspire you to your highest and best. Beauty draws the very best out of you and unites you with the highest. The beauty that is within you cannot be contained, so let it shine forth. Fill your heart and mind with beautiful thoughts, and reflect Me, for I AM beauty. Look for the beauty in everything, and when you look deeply enough and long enough, you will see it. Rise above the sordid and ugly things in life, for by rising above them, you can help to transform and transmute them. Beauty is in the eye of the beholder; therefore it is deep within you. Go forth this day determined to see beauty in everyone and everything, and you will do so. Love and beauty go hand in hand, so let My universal love flow freely in and through you, bringing unity and oneness.

AR too many souls waste time and energy blaming the wrongs in the world on everyone else instead of recognising that they can do something about it when they start within themselves. Start putting your own house in order first. When a stone is thrown into the centre of a pond, the ripples go out and out; but they start from that stone; they start from that centre. Start with yourself; then you can radiate peace, love, harmony and understanding out to all souls around you. Get into action now. You long to see a better world; then do something about it, not by pointing your finger at everyone else but by looking within, searching your heart, righting your own wrongs and finding the answer within yourself. Then you can move forward with authority and be a real help to your neighbour and to all those souls you contact. Change starts with the individual, then goes out into the community, the town, the nation and the world.

EVERYTHING has to grow and expand. You would not want to remain a child all of your life, having to be fed and dressed and have everything done for you. If you watch a child, you will see how it wants to change and how it wants to try new things. All the time it is experimenting and learning, growing and expanding. This is the natural process of growing up, of changing. A child does not have to struggle to do it; it comes quite naturally. So with the unfolding of the New Age, which is right here with you now. You need not fight and struggle to move into it; you need not fear the unknown; you need not be concerned with the speed of the changes and expansion all around you. Look forward with real joy and expectancy to what is waiting to unfold. Nothing is too great, nothing is too wonderful, nothing is impossible. See My wonders unfold in true perfection, and give eternal thanks.

*Y*OU can help to bring down My heaven on earth when you realise that I AM leading you and showing you the way. You will find all the directions deep within you, so you cannot possibly be led astray or take the wrong route. Seek within and follow those directions, and behold wonder upon wonder come about. There can never be a dull moment when I AM guiding and directing you. Seek Me and find Me at all times. You do not have to look very far; I AM there in the very midst of you, but you have to be consciously aware of Me. As you live and move and have your being in Me, you are creating the new heaven and new earth. There is no strain in creation. I said, 'Let there be Light,' and there was Light. I say, 'Behold My new heaven and new earth.' Therefore behold it, give eternal thanks for it, and dwell in it in perfect love, peace and harmony now.

MANY souls are seeking an answer to all the chaos and confusion in the world at this time. Day by day it grows worse, but be not afraid, for things will have to get worse before they can get better. A boil comes to a head before it bursts, and then all the poisons are released and are cleared away. Things have to come to a head in the world before the poisons of hate, greed, jealousy and selfishness are released and healing can take place. I need you at perfect peace within. You will find it as you keep your mind stayed on Me and can raise your consciousness, seeing only the very best. You cannot help the world situation if you allow yourself to become involved in it. You have to be immune to the disease or you too will contract it, and then you can be of no help whatsoever. I need your help. I need you free. I need you at perfect peace. Then I can use you.

SEE that everything you do is dedicated to Me and is of benefit to the whole. When you live for the whole, the self is forgotten in service to your fellow human beings, and when you are serving them, you are serving Me. All is so closely intertwined that you cannot separate one from the other, I in you and you in Me. I AM in everything and everyone; therefore I AM in your neighbour, in your friend and in your enemy alike. Wherever I AM, there is love, for I AM love. Fill your heart and mind with love, for everything and everyone responds to love, as love draws the very best out of all. Where love is, there My Spirit is, and where My Spirit is, there is the source of your spiritual life. Seek always that which is deep within you, and waste no more time seeking for the answer to life from without.

*Y*OU must learn to stand on your own feet and find your own individual path to function in the overall plan. Draw only from Me, the source of all life and all creation; then you cannot go wrong. Never waver when the going becomes difficult, but simply go steadily forward, knowing that it is but a rough patch you are moving through. The quicker you move through it the better, with as little resistance and resentment as possible, learning important and necessary lessons every step of the way. You must learn to hold on, to be very patient and persistent, and not to give up easily. Hold the vision before you. Know where you are going and what it is that has to be achieved, and then never let it go until you have seen it brought about. You cannot be faint-hearted in this life. It calls for that inner strength and knowing which nothing can shatter or throw off balance. Let your strength and security be in Me.

DO not just talk about the new heaven and new earth; it is up to you to bring it down into your life to make it reality. Do not talk about love and loving; live it so that all can see what it means. Words without action are meaningless and useless. They are like hot air that evaporates into nothingness. You are to bring down My kingdom on earth by the way you live and behave, so your life is an example, a joyous example, which all will want to follow. No one wants to go through life over-burdened, lacking joy and spontaneity. Blessed is that person who brings joy to those souls who are burdened and lack sparkle in life. Cast all your burdens upon Me, and bring joy and freedom to all those souls you contact. Be joy and inspiration, and reflect Me in all that you do, say and think. Be at perfect peace as you do My will and walk in My ways, glorifying Me.

EXPECT only the very best, and expect every need to be met, even the most seemingly impossible. Never at any time limit yourself or feel that you should not expect too much. See your needs very clearly, voice them, and then have complete faith and confidence that they will be met. How it will come about will have to be left in My hands. I have to work through channels to bring it about, but all things are possible with Me. So let go and see My wonders and glories come about, give eternal thanks, and use everything for the good of the whole at all times. You are not living by human laws but by divine laws; therefore anything can happen at any time. Expect miracles, and see them take place. Hold ever before you the thought of prosperity and abundance, and know that doing so sets into operation forces that will bring it into being. The more positive you are, the quicker will it all come about.

HY try to seek guidance through anyone else? Why not come directly to Me? Do you not know that I AM within you? Do you not know that I AM here to answer all questions, to help solve all problems, and to guide and direct your every step if you will only let Me? I never push Myself on anyone. You must choose to seek and find Me, and when you do, I AM here waiting to take over, waiting to pour love in and through you, waiting to show you the way. Once you have made your choice and allowed Me to take the helm, you can let go and simply follow out My instructions step by step. You will see My wonders and glories come about, and see miracle upon miracle take place in your life. You will know that when something is right and has My full blessings, nothing and no one can stand in the way, for it will come about at the right time in true perfection.

ALL that I have is yours. Think of the wonder of those words, and then let your consciousness expand so that you can accept them and know the true meaning of them. See them become reality in your life, and never again accept any limitations, for all My promises will come about; they are not vain promises. Simply hold on in faith, and never at any time let your faith waver. Everything comes to those souls who wait upon Me and put their whole faith and trust in Me. Behold wonder upon wonder unfold before you. Recognise the wonder in the little things in life as well as the big ones. Open your eyes so that you miss nothing; open your heart and keep the love flowing. Love attracts love. Every soul longs to be loved, so why not give love; and as you give so shall you receive. But learn to give freely without any strings attached, and enjoy life to the full.

WAKE up and live! Live that full and glorious life which is your true heritage. Be afraid of nothing. You have within you all wisdom, all power, all strength and all understanding. Pluck out those weeds of doubt, fear and uncertainty so that they cannot choke the beautiful garden deep within you, and all the very best is allowed to grow in true freedom and perfection. Release that which is within so that it is reflected without; you cannot hide it no matter how hard you may try to do so. If there is chaos and confusion within you, it will be reflected in the outer world by the way you look, the way you behave, by the things you do and by what you have around you. You cannot hide what is within no matter how hard you try. When your thoughts are of the highest, beauty and perfection are reflected without. You are like a mirror which has been highly polished; nothing can remain hidden.

GO through life with a great sense of peace, and you will be amazed how much you can get done. You can do far more in quietness and confidence than in a disturbed state of mind. When you are unable to concentrate on what you are doing, it means that you are doing it in a half-hearted manner, and therefore not to the very best of your ability. You see how important your right attitude is to everything you do, so that you can enjoy life to the full. I want you to enjoy life and to find the very best in life. You will find that when you know where you are going and what you are doing, you do not waste any time being indecisive, but can go straight ahead and do it. Take time to find out directly from Me what is required of you. You can only do it in the peace and stillness, so find time for it. It is a very important key.

OW is the time of building, of creating, of unity and harmony, of peace and love, of wholeness and oneness. Hold these positive, constructive, creative thoughts in your consciousness all the time, and never let them go. See them live and move and have their being in you, and behold the vision of the new heaven and the new earth take form and substance. Let it unfold within you. As you become attuned to the idea of the New Age and to the true meaning of it, it will gradually begin to unfold within you, and you will realise that you are part of it and it is part of you. It is something tremendous, like a slumbering giant waiting to awaken from its sleep, and once it begins to stir, nothing will be able to stop its coming forth. There is nothing to fight against; there is no need to struggle any longer. Simply learn to wait upon Me, and let My perfect plan unfold.

AM within you. I AM not more in one soul than in another; it is simply a matter of awareness. Some souls are more aware of the divinity within them than others and are able to draw from that source and live by that source. Therefore they appear to be living and demonstrating something supernatural. There is nothing supernatural about it; it is simply living by My laws, using the power that is within each one as it should be used. Air is there to be breathed, but it is up to you to breathe it in. Electricity is there to be used, but it has to be harnessed and then switched on and used. Otherwise the electricity is there but it does not demonstrate its power which is waiting to be released. So with the spiritual power within you. It is there for you to use, but unless you plug in and switch on that power, there it remains.

WHEN you refuse to learn a lesson one way, it will be presented to you in another way. There is always the easy way, but when you refuse to accept it, the more difficult and complicated way will be presented to you. Why not learn your lessons the easy way? Why not be like a little child, eager and receptive to all that is taking place in your life, and unfold with it all in the most natural way? That is My plan for you, so why make life difficult for yourself when it is not necessary? It only holds up progress when you do. You will find, as you learn to put Me first before all else, that everything will fall into place perfectly. When you can raise your consciousness and keep it raised to a spiritual level in life, to what matters, then vast changes will take place and life will unfold for you without any effort. Life is very simple. Why make it complicated for yourself?

RAY without ceasing. Let your life be a constant prayer of love and thanksgiving. Life is very, very good, but always remember that life is what you make it. Therefore, if you are negative, you draw negativity towards you, and a dark cloud comes over your life, separating you from that highest good. If you are constantly positive, seeing the good in everything and everyone, there is blue sky and sunshine all around you and within you. Fill your life with love, faith, hope and fulfilment. Learn to love life, for when you do, your life is a constant prayer and you do indeed pray without ceasing. Prayer is your inner communion with Me, when we walk and talk together as we did in the beginning. Prayer is the food of the Spirit, the nourisher of the soul. It is a deep inner need in every soul. Feel that inner need and answer it.

HEN I tell you that My glorious plan will unfold step by step, you may visualise it all happening slowly. My beloved, nothing will happen slowly now. Everything is being speeded up. Nevertheless, it will be an unfoldment because all will come about in perfect timing. Let it come and do not try to stop anything taking place because you are afraid of the speed with which it is coming. My timing is perfect. Why not accept it? Let there be no resistance in you, but find perfect freedom and joy as the plan unfolds. It is a truly wonderful plan, and you are part of it. You have your own part to play in it; that is why it is important to find out what your part is, and for you to do it now. Do not drift through another day without finding out. When you take time to be still, in the silence you will know what is your specific part.

GIVE constant thanks for everything. There is much to be grateful for; open your eyes, look around, and see how blessed you are. As you do so, you will find yourself filled with an overwhelming feeling of love and gratitude, and the whole of life and living will take on a new meaning. The people around you will mean more to you because your heart is filled with love for them, and you have a deeper understanding and tolerance towards them. You will find yourself grateful for them, for their love and companionship, for just being themselves. Your eyes will be open to all the beauty and harmony around you, to the wonders of nature. You will see with eyes that really see; you will hear with ears that really hear; and you will speak with words of love and understanding. Life will be good for you because you are taking nothing for granted, but are appreciative of everything and can see My hand in everything.

*Y*OUR positive, creative, loving thoughts hold a tremendous power, far greater than you realise, for thoughts are power. Therefore banish all negative thoughts. Always look on the bright side of life, for the more joy and love you radiate, the more joy and love will you draw to you. Love all those souls around you, for you will find everyone responds to love in the end. Children and animals respond immediately because they have no barriers to pull down. They feel that love flow instinctively, for they are not suspicious of wrong motives and intentions, but simply accept and respond to love and return it joyously; whereas so often adults are suspicious and imagine that there must be some ulterior motive. Never allow suspicion of your motives to close your heart towards anyone. When those motives are pure and genuine, let the love flow in full force until all barriers have been knocked down. Love is the key to life. You hold that key within you.

I was shown a field of ripe corn ready to be harvested. I heard the words:

There is a right time and season for everything. Never put off until tomorrow what you know you should do now, but flow with the rhythm of all life and be at perfect peace.

ET into tune with Me in the peace and stillness. How can you expect to hear My still, small voice when you are in turmoil within and are too busy to take time to be still and listen? As you learn to be still, you will be able to do it, no matter what you are doing and no matter where you are. You will be able to pull your cloak of peace and stillness around you and find that centre of peace which nothing can disturb. There you will find Me in the very midst of you. You will find your realisation of oneness with Me, the source of all creation. In this state of peace and oneness you will be in full command of every situation, and you will know exactly what to do and how to do it. It is something all individuals can do when they want to; it is not reserved just for the few. Why not be still now and be at perfect peace?

EARN to act spontaneously, to act by intuition, and to do what your heart prompts you to do, not just what your mind tells you is reasonable or sensible. Some acts of pure love may appear to be very unreasonable, even foolish, in the eyes of others but it matters not. When you are prompted to act, do so and do not stop to weigh it up or even wonder why you are doing it. That small act of love may have some very far-reaching effect. It may not even reveal itself to begin with. Do not waste time looking for results; simply do what you know you must do, and then leave the rest to Me. Sometimes it may take a long time for that seed of love to germinate in a hard, cold heart, but once it has been planted, sooner or later it will show itself. All you have to do is to do your part in faith, and know that all is very, very well.

WHEN one door closes, another one opens. Expect that new door to reveal even greater wonders and glories and surprises. Always expect the very best from every situation, and see the very best come out of each one. Never become depressed or despondent as you see one door close in your face. Simply know that all things work together for good for those souls who truly love Me and put Me first in everything. Feel yourself grow and expand as you go through every experience, and look for the reason for it. Learn by it, and be determined never to make the same mistake twice, if you have made a seeming mistake, for much can come out of it when you do not allow it to get you down. Your whole attitude towards life is very important; therefore realise that life is what you make it. Make it a wonderful, joyous, exciting life where anything can happen at any moment because you are doing My will.

WHY not start each day by getting into tune with the highest good within you? Then carry it forth into everything you do throughout the day. Let peace and love flow freely in and through you, out to all you contact. See My wholeness and perfection in all your fellow human beings, and dwell on that. When you can do so, all imperfections in them will be eliminated, and you will behold them in the light of perfection; for you will be seeing with My eyes, and I see only the perfect in everything and everyone. Reflect Me; be at one with Me. Let your consciousness be of oneness and of wholeness. Know that I AM working in and through you and that your every thought and action is guided and directed by Me. Know that as harmony, beauty, and law and order enter your life, chaos and confusion fly out the window. As long as you remain in that state of consciousness, all will be very, very well.

KEEP your standards high; the higher the better. Be not careless or slapdash about anything you undertake. Perfection must always be the aim. It may be seemingly impossible to reach, but nevertheless go on reaching, go on stretching. Never be satisfied with anything mediocre, or anything that is done half-heartedly and without love. Let all you do, whatever it may be, be done to My honour and glory, for when your aim is to do everything for Me, your aim will always be of the very highest, and you will not be satisfied unless you are giving of your very best. Learn to forget the self in service to others. You will find real joy in giving on every level. Always remember, there are many different levels on which you can give, from the highest to the lowest, from the spiritual to the physical. Whatever level it may be, give and give whole-heartedly, and you will find that as you give, so will you receive.

BE still and receptive to life. The more still you can become, the more receptive you are, for it is in the stillness that you can hear My still, small voice. It is in the stillness that you become aware of My wonders all around you. You become very sensitive to the things that matter in life, and in this state of sensitivity doors can be flung wide open and anything can happen. You must seek and find periods of peace and stillness, no matter how busy a person you are, for they need not be long periods. You will find those few moments in silent communion with Me will work wonders in everything you do. Instead of rushing into a project, or doing something because it has to be done, your whole attitude towards whatever you undertake will be one of benediction, praise and thanksgiving. Because your attitude and approach are right, only the very best can come from it and bring blessings to all those souls concerned with it.

WALK in the light and never be afraid to let the light of truth be beamed fully on you. When you have nothing to hide, nothing to be ashamed of, you are as free as a very small child who has no inhibitions and expresses itself with real joy. It bubbles over with joy, and that joy is infectious, radiating to all who come into contact with it. Joy cannot be hidden or contained. It reveals itself in a hundred and one ways: in a look, a word, an expression. Joy draws people to it, for everyone responds to joyous, happy souls and enjoys being in their company. Joy draws souls to it like steel to a magnet, whereas misery and negativity repel. When you know you are doing the right thing and are in the right place, you radiate joy and freedom. Everything flows smoothly for you and falls into its rightful place. You draw the very best to you; you cannot help doing so, for like attracts like.

AS you learn to do My will and walk in My ways, you will begin to know the meaning of peace and harmony within. Your heart will overflow with love, your understanding will expand and you will become more tolerant and open, and see clearly that there are many paths which lead to Me. You will learn to live and let live, and no longer feel that your way is the only way. You will never again be dogmatic about anything, but very quietly and confidently go your way doing what you feel is right for you. You will no longer try to change other souls, but will learn to live in such a way that others will want to know what it is you have got that they have not. Never forget, you can teach far more by example. If you quietly go about doing My will, it will have far more effect on humanity than shouting many wonderful words from the roof-tops and failing to live what you preach.

ALWAYS take the optimistic outlook over everything, and banish all gloom and negativity. You are surrounded by many wonderful people, things and experiences in life. Why not concentrate on them and give thanks for them, letting go and releasing all that is unpleasant, unhappy or difficult? By your attitude and outlook you draw to you the very best or the very worst in life. Therefore, if you are blaming your circumstances, life or people for your misfortunes, look within to see what you can do to change your attitude. As you start doing it, little by little you will find changes taking place, and you will begin to realise how mightily blessed you are and how truly wonderful life is. What a joy and a privilege it is to be alive, to be where you are, doing what you are doing, surrounded by so many wonderful things and people! Start right now looking for them. They are right there, so you will not have to look very far.

DO you want to do something to help the world situation? Then look within, for never forget that it all starts in the individual. As you change your consciousness to love, peace, harmony and unity, the consciousness of the whole world will change. But it is not always very pleasant when you start doing it. You will find dark spots which need to be cleared within yourself. You will find that your motives are not always of the highest and that your likes and dislikes are far more pronounced than you imagined. You will find that you are very inclined to discriminate when there should be no discrimination, for all are one in My sight. You will find that your love for one another is not all it should be. Start putting all your cards on the table, and be determined to do something about it, and start doing it now. There is no better time. I AM here to help you. Call upon Me, and let Me guide your every step.

RE you in harmony with all life? Do you feel at one with all those souls around you, and at peace? Are you part of the chaos and confusion in the world at this time, or is your life part of the answer to world problems? There can be no sitting on the fence at this time. You are either working for the light or you are not; the choice is in your hands. You are either with Me or against Me. Your faith and belief cannot be lukewarm or half-hearted. It must be whole-hearted or not at all. I need you aflame, on fire with love for Me, completely dedicated to Me and to My work, willing to do My will no matter what the cost. I ask for all, and only when all is given will you receive all. Nothing shall be withheld from you, and you will know that all I have is yours.

*Y*OU cannot do all you should be doing when you are strained. Take time to be alone, and do something simple, something you enjoy doing, but let it be of your own choosing, not something someone else has suggested. As you do it, you will find yourself able to see everything from a different level of consciousness. The weight will be lifted, and you will find you will be able to do far more. Also, never try to look too far ahead; that in itself can cause great strain and distress. You can only take one step at a time, so take that one step, and the next will follow at exactly the right time. Let life unfold, and do not try to manipulate it. Do not get annoyed and impatient when things do not work out quite as you had expected they would. Instead, look for and see the purpose and plan running through all that is taking place, and realise that all is for the very best.

*L*EARN to think and feel for others, to do unto others as you would have them do unto you. Learn to understand and enter fully into their lives and hearts, pouring out love and understanding to them, thereby banishing all criticism, judgement and condemnation. Realise that love transforms and transmutes all bitterness and hatred and that understanding opens up hearts that have been closed and have remained cold and unresponsive. Put into practice in your life those words, 'Resist not evil but overcome evil with good.' It is easier said than done, but until it is done and lived, there cannot be peace and goodwill to all humanity. These words have been heard, read and preached down the ages, but they have not been lived; that is why there are wars, destruction, evil and hatred in the world. It will go on until humanity learns to live a life and not just talk about it, learns to make these wonderful words live and vibrate in everyday life.

S you contribute your specific gifts and talents to the whole, so is each piece of the jigsaw puzzle of life put together forming the perfect whole. What are your specific gifts or talents? Why not share them and cease hiding them away, for they are all needed. You may feel you have many gifts, or you may feel you have little or nothing to give. This latter is not so. You have your own unique something to give which no one else can give, and that something is needed. It is up to you to find out what it is and give it. It takes all sorts to make up the whole. Every tiny screw, cog and spring is needed to make a clock. Every organ of the body, every tiny cell and atom is needed to make up the whole perfect body. When you can see yourself as part of the whole, you will no longer want to withhold what you have to give.

IF you find it difficult to love your fellow human beings, do not try and force yourself to do it, for you cannot make yourself love someone. But as you seek Me and My help, I will place that seed of love in your heart. Then all you have to do is very gently and quietly to tend it and watch it grow without any effort on your part. To try and will yourself to love someone is a losing battle. You will find that like will attract like, that you will quite naturally be drawn towards some people more than others, and that you will be able to blend in more easily with each other; but let it not concern you. Gradually you will know the meaning of universal love as you grow spiritually and come to know the meaning of My divine love. Let it unfold very naturally without any effort on your part, but just a deep inner longing to love more.

*Y*OUR attitude is vitally important, far more important than you realise. Therefore if you cannot do something with the right attitude, don't do it at all until you can change your attitude. Really enjoy doing it, and realise that, whatever it is, it is important to the smooth running of the whole. Never be afraid to shoulder your responsibilities, but grow in wisdom and stature as you do so. Know that you are never given more than you are able to stand. It is important that each responsibility helps you to stretch and expand that little bit more. The object of responsibilities is not to weigh you down and overburden you, but to help you to grow. Do not resent the responsibilities you are given, but be grateful for them. Know that you would not be given them if I did not feel you were capable of shouldering them. Seek My help at all times. I AM your ever-ready help and guide. Call upon Me.

*L*EARN to be very flexible and adaptable. At the same time, always work from a stable inner knowing, so that you are not influenced by or dependent upon outer circumstances and conditions. Realise that your outer life and living are a reflection of your inner life. When you are at peace within, you radiate peace without, for when your heart is overflowing with love, you cannot help but reflect and radiate that love all around you. You cannot hide that which is deep within you, for your outer state is a mirror of your inner state. The time you spend in peace and stillness is never wasted. It is necessary for every soul to find time to be still and reflect on that which is deep within, on the things that matter in life, that make your life what it is, the ways of the Spirit. It matters not how busy your day may be. Those times of stillness are essential and are the very backbone of your life.

BE not bowed down by self-concern, so that you miss all the wonders in life. Dwell on all the beauty and wonders in life. Go about with your eyes wide open and appreciate the beauty around you. Take one day at a time and appreciate that day to the full. Let every moment be filled with love and thanksgiving. When anything comes up which is inharmonious, look around quickly and see how it can be exchanged for something which is harmonious. Do it quickly because negative and detrimental thoughts can grow as fast as weeds in a garden and choke all beautiful and delicate plants if they are allowed to take control. Learn to control your thoughts so they are only ones of beauty, harmony and love. Once your positive thoughts have been well established, you will automatically look for the very best in every situation. Only then can you relax, let go and enter the joy and freedom of the Spirit.

HY not start right now receiving your spiritual inspiration and guidance at first hand and not through anyone else? Do you not realise that you have within you all wisdom, all knowledge, all understanding? You do not have to seek it without, but it does mean that you have to take time to be still and to go deep within to find it. There is nothing more wonderful or worthwhile than direct contact with Me, the source of all creation. It means you have to take time, and if necessary make time to find it. You have to reach the stage where you are consciously aware of Me and of My divine presence at all times, where you are willing to bring Me into the whole of your life, and walk and talk with Me all the time, sharing everything with me, both your successes and your failures. When the love is flowing and you are one with Me, you will want more than anything to share everything with Me.

EVERY soul has to learn self-discipline, and the earlier it is learnt in life, the easier it is. To begin with, self-discipline can be a real effort because you have to make yourself do things which the lower self kicks against. You have to learn to say 'no' to yourself, but the firmer you are with yourself, the more quickly will peace reign within. It is good every now and again to take yourself in hand and see where you are being weak and self-indulgent. It means that you have to be very honest and not make excuses for yourself. It may even help you to write down the places where you feel you need to change so you have them there before you. Then do something about them. If you feel incapable of overcoming certain weaknesses, I do not ask you to do it on your own. I AM always here to help you. Why not call upon Me?

EVERYONE has had the experience of being thrown completely off-balance by something someone has said or done. Instead of facing it straight away, you may have allowed it to take hold of you and affect your whole outlook, until you found yourself tied up in knots and no good to anyone. You may have even started the day with the very best intentions, with love in your heart for everyone, determined to see the very best everywhere you look. Next time it happens to you, recognise what is happening and immediately raise your consciousness. Call upon Me. Let your mind be stayed upon Me, so that you become consciously aware of Me and My divine presence. See what a difference it will make to you. If you can quickly turn your thoughts to Me and to My divine love when you find yourself in a negative situation, everything can change completely. Remember this idea next time. Try it and see how it works.

T matters not where you are or what you are doing; I AM with you always. But unless you are consciously aware of it, you can go through life like a blind person, unaware of the wonders and beauties all around you, groping your way in the darkness. When you are aware, you have eyes to see with and ears to hear with. All the little things in life have a new and deeper meaning. You take nothing for granted, but see a plan and purpose running through everything that is taking place in your life. You find a real joy and uplift in everything that is happening to you. You see with the eyes of the Spirit. You understand the things that matter in life, and life is full to overflowing with joy and happiness. You begin to appreciate that there is nothing haphazard in all that is going on. You recognise My hand in everything, and your heart is filled with love and gratitude.

*L*ET the power of the Spirit flow in and through you. Open yourself up to this infinite power; and realise its true secret lies in keeping in close contact with Me, in drawing from the infinite, eternal source. It is always here to be drawn upon by all souls who are ready to use it aright for the benefit of the whole. You have to be ready; you have to ask before you can receive. It will not be pushed upon you before you are prepared. Do you believe that with Me all things are possible? Do you accept it as a fact, or do you still allow doubts and fears to spoil the perfection of your life? There is a perfect rhythm in all life, and when you are in rhythm you flow with it without any effort, and find joy and upliftment in so doing. So why not get into rhythm, get into tune and enjoy life to the full?

SEARCH your heart. Is there anything in you which is causing disunity and division? Is there any misunderstanding, jealousy, envy or anything negative which may be putting on the brakes? You will have to face yourself fairly and squarely and be honest with yourself. You will know without a shadow of doubt if you happen to be that piece of grit which is holding up the perfect outworking of My plan. If you feel uncomfortable and find yourself making excuses and trying to justify your actions and your thoughts, you may be sure there is something deep within you that needs to be changed. When you recognise it, do not allow it to weigh you down, but start right there and then to change your whole outlook and attitude. I AM always here to help you. Call on Me, and I will help you to overcome all that seems to stand in your way, preventing you from feeling at one with the whole.

NEVER at any time feel that you have nothing to give. You have a tremendous amount to give, and you will find that the less you think about it, the better it will work out. The more you are thinking and living for others and can forget the self completely in service to others, with never a thought of what you can get out of life, the happier you will be. Never give with one hand and take away with the other. When you give something, whatever it may be, give it with no strings attached, so that it can be used completely freely. When you give, let your giving be done abundantly, freely and whole-heartedly, and then forget about it. This principle applies to gifts on all levels, whether material or spiritual, tangible or intangible. Always be generous in your giving, and never be afraid of suffering lack, for if you do, it is not true giving. With true giving, you will lack nothing.

YOU have a tremendous work to do. It is the silent work of creating more love in the world. It is like the yeast in a lump of dough which does its work very quietly and without any fuss, and yet without it the bread would be a solid lump. Therefore love those souls you are with, love what you are doing, love your environment, and love those souls who are your seeming enemies. There is far more grace in loving the seemingly unlovable than in simply loving those souls who love you. Feel the need for love in every soul, and allow yourself to become a channel for love to flow through to meet that need. As each individual learns to love for love's sake, so will the heaviness in the world be lightened, for love brings an element of lightness where there was heaviness and darkness. Love starts in each individual, so look within your own heart and draw it forth. Give of it freely and with real joy.

*G*IVE thanks for everything. Keep your heart wide open and let your feeling of gratitude pour forth in an unending stream. There is so much to be grateful for. Gratitude keeps your eyes open to Me and to My wonders. Therefore you miss nothing and you see Me in all that is taking place. You know there is a pattern and plan running through your life; therefore nothing is by chance. Every contact is right, every action guided. You must have complete faith to be able to live in this way, faith that your life is being guided and directed by Me. It means you first have to surrender your all to Me to use as I will. You must learn that only when you give all do you receive all. You can only do it when you have learnt to love Me with all your heart, mind, soul and strength; for without love you cannot take these steps, you cannot live this life. So open your heart and love.

*L*EARNING to put first things first is vitally important, for only when first things are put first will all work out perfectly. Search your heart and see what you are putting first. Is it yourself and your own welfare? Is it your job and your material circumstances? Are you content to go through life completely unaware of Me, confident that you can get along just as well without My help and that you have no need of Me? You are absolutely free to adopt any attitude you wish. No one will stop you. But you must be willing to take the consequences when things go wrong. Remember, when you know what is right and choose to go your own way, the responsibility you hold is even greater, for you cannot plead ignorance. Never make the excuse that there is so much to do that there is not time to fit everything in. I tell you that when you put first things first, there is time for everything.

*Y*OU must do your own work in this spiritual life. I AM always here to help those souls who help themselves, but you have to take the first step. You will never learn lessons if everything is done for you. You cannot train a child by doing everything for it. You have to let it do things for itself. No matter how slow or fumbling its actions are to begin with, you have to stand back and be very patient. Very patiently and very lovingly I have to stand back and see you do your own work and make mistakes. But always remember, you will benefit by your mistakes; nothing is in vain. All the time you are learning new lessons and advancing along the spiritual path. Every step, no matter how small, takes you nearer the goal, your realisation of oneness with me; until eventually you realise there is no separation, and all is one, and you are part of that one glorious life.

DO you sometimes wonder why you are where you are, doing what you are doing? Do you ever have doubts in your mind? Seek deep within your heart, and answer these questions honestly. Then, if you feel you are still one of those Doubting Thomases, take time to be still, to seek enlightenment from within, and find out where you fit into the whole vast scheme. I can assure you that it is not by chance that you are where you are. Life may have been very tough for you. You may have had to go through many tests and trials. You may even have been plunged into the fiery furnace. You may be sure there is a reason for all of it: so that all the dross might be burnt away and nothing but the pure gold—the I AM within —remains, and so that I can work in and through the I AM to bring about My wonders and glories for all to see.

To learn the laws of manifestation, there are vitally important lessons —patience, persistence and perseverance. You have to learn implicit obedience and be willing to follow out My instructions, no matter how foolish they may appear to be. It is only when these lessons have been learnt and put into practice that the most wonderful things begin to happen in your life, and you do indeed behold My laws being lived and demonstrated. Always remember, you have to do something, you have to live a life and not just spend your life praying, hoping something will happen. Prayer is necessary, but it is not enough. You have to learn to live a life for all to see. Talking about faith is not enough. You have to live in such a way that all those souls around you can see what it means to live by faith, what it means to put your whole faith and trust in Me, the Lord your God, the divinity within you.

I was shown a deep, dark well and on top was a bucket with a rope attached to it. I saw the bucket being lowered into the well, and when it was drawn up out of the darkness, it was filled to the brim with pure, clear water. I heard the words:

Deep within every soul is purity of Spirit. Take time to seek for it until you find it, and then draw it forth.

*Y*OU can soar to great heights with a heart filled with praise and thanksgiving. But like the tiny lark, you have to take off from the ground, you have to make that special effort. It need not be a strain; it can be a joyous, light-hearted effort. Why remain anchored, when action on your part can change your life completely? Set your sights high, the higher the better. Expect the most wonderful happenings, not in the future but right now. Stride forward with a firm, steady step, knowing with a deep, certain inner knowing that you will reach every goal you set yourself. Why not take some positive action today? Why not start the wheels turning? Once you have done your part, you will receive all the help you require, but not until then. Have confidence in your ability to do all things because you are drawing your substance from Me. You can do all things when your faith and trust are in Me.

WHEN your desire is to bring peace and harmony into the world, then you will have to start by finding peace and harmony within your own heart. It is a waste of time talking about peace. You have to seek and find that consciousness of peace which nothing and no one can disturb, and remain in it. In that state of consciousness you will be able to be effective and help to bring peace and harmony into the lives of the many. Be consciously aware of peace and harmony in your own life first and, like a stone thrown into the middle of a pond, the ripples will spread out and out, touching and changing the lives of many. 'As you sow, so shall you reap.' When you sow discord and disharmony, you reap discord and disharmony; whereas when you sow peace and harmony, the harvest of peace and harmony shall be great, not just for you, but for all those souls with whom you come into contact.

GIVE and go on giving. Never try to hoard anything. Keep everything flowing freely. Whether it is talent, love, money or possessions, keep it flowing, keep it moving. When you do, you will find it will increase a thousandfold. The life force in your body cannot be hoarded; it has to keep moving, keep circulating; for only in this way can newer, fresher and even greater life force enter, and you can become a vital being. So it is with everything: keep it moving, and never hold up the flow. Watch life unfold for you in true perfection. See your every need met at exactly the right time. Expect it to come about, and never allow any doubts into your consciousness. Be positive about everything, no matter what the outer conditions may appear to be, and feel those niggardly thoughts disappearing as they are replaced by increase and plenty. Have absolute faith that all is very, very well, and all is working out perfectly because all is in My hands.

HOLD the vision of perfection, harmony and beauty ever before you, and see it in everything and everyone. Let the love within you bubble over like water and flow to all alike. Let there be no discrimination in you, for all are of Me; all are one family. Universal love starts within each individual and works its way out. When each individual realises it and allows that love to flow freely, great changes will come about in the world, for it is love that transmutes all hatred, jealousy, envy, criticism and greed. These are the qualities that cause war, destruction and death. Love creates life—life everlasting, life abundant. Love brings with it peace, joy, and true and lasting happiness and contentment. Above all, it brings unity and oneness. So if you have wandered off into the highways and byways and lost your way, come back to the path of love which leads straight to Me, and there you will find Me waiting deep within you.

WHEN you choose to do My will and walk in My ways, you have to do it whole-heartedly, no matter what it may mean. You have to take the rough with the smooth when learning that vital lesson of instant obedience to My will. Only when you give all will you receive all. In this spiritual life you cannot pick out all the plums and leave the cake; it is all or nothing. Many souls like to choose the parts in this life that appeal to them and to ignore those parts that do not comply with their baser desires. Doing so is not living a spiritual life; it is picking and choosing what you want to do, not what I require of you. You cannot expect things to work out for you if that is your attitude. I need your total surrender and dedication before I can work wonders and miracles in and through you. Now that you know, why not do something about it?

IVE one day at a time. Do not try and rush ahead, making arrangements for tomorrow, for tomorrow may never come. Enjoy today to the full; enjoy it as if it were your last. Do all the wonderful things you have longed to do, not recklessly or thoughtlessly, but with real joy. Be like a small child who takes no thought for tomorrow and has forgotten what happened yesterday, but just lives as if the only time that matters is now. The now is the most exciting time you have ever known, so do not miss a second of it. Live on the tips of your toes, ready for anything to happen at any moment. When you live this way, you are ready and open for anything that may take place. Changes will come and they will come very quickly. Lift up your heart in deep gratitude as they come along one by one. Always see the very best in every change that takes place.

NEXT time you are faced with a job which does not appeal to you, take time before you even start it to change your complete outlook towards it. See yourself doing it for Me, and if your love for Me is what it should be, you will find a real joy and delight in doing whatever it is perfectly. What is more, you will find you have plenty of time to do everything that has to be done. Never waste time convincing yourself that you do not have the time and are far too busy. Simply go ahead and do what has to be done. Let your life run smoothly and peacefully without any sense of rush. When you start the day aright, with a heart full of love and gratitude and with a feeling of expectancy that it will be a wonderful day with everything falling perfectly into place, you will draw it all to you.

ET Me work in and through you. Let My love and light flow freely in and through you out into the world. Realise that this is as it was in the beginning, when we walked and talked together, and that you have gone the full cycle and have once again returned and become one with Me, the Beloved. Do not dream about it; do not long for it to be so; simply know that it is so now and that no longer is there any separation. No longer do you have to wander in the wilderness lost and alone, not knowing which way to turn. Realise that your every step is guided and directed by Me, and that as you become more and more aware of Me, of My divine presence, you can never again lose your way. So give eternal thanks and let your heart be so full of joy and gratitude that you express it at all times, and your every breath says, 'Thank you, Beloved.'

WHEN a soul intends to get as much out of life as possible without giving, that soul cannot find real and lasting happiness and joy; for it is in thinking of and living for others that one finds deep inner joy and contentment. No one can live unto themselves and be happy. Whenever you find yourself with a feeling of discontent and dissatisfaction in life, you may be sure it is because you have stopped thinking of others and have become too wrapped up in yourself. The way to change is to start thinking of someone else and do something for them so that the self is completely forgotten. There are so many souls in need that there is always something you can do for someone else. So why not open your eyes and open your heart, and let light show you the way, let love guide your actions. Let my love infil and enfold you, and be at perfect peace.

WHEN you plant a seed in the ground, it may look like any other seed, brown and dried up with the appearance of no life force in it. Nevertheless, you place it in the ground in confidence, and at the right time it starts to grow. It knows what it is going to grow into. You only know what you have placed in the ground by what was on the packet, but you have confidence that the specific plant will grow from that specific seed, and it does. When you plant the right ideas and thoughts in your mind, you must do it in complete confidence, knowing that only the perfect will spring forth from those ideas and thoughts. As your trust and confidence become strong and unshakable, those constructive thoughts and ideas begin to grow and develop. In this way you can accomplish anything. It is that inner power within each one which does the work. It is the I AM within you.

NTIL you start to put what you are learning into practice, you do not know whether or not it works for you. It may work for others, but what about you? Remember, you cannot bask in somebody else's deep inner spiritual experiences. It helps to read about them, to learn about them, and even to hear and talk about them. But it is up to you to live them and practise them in your own life if you desire to live by the Spirit, to live by faith. No one can make you live this life. Every soul is absolutely free to make its own choice. What have you chosen to do? Just sit back and spend the rest of your life listening to other people's experiences? Or are you going to start right here and now living a life fully dedicated to Me, putting into practice all those wonderful lessons you have been learning, and seeing how they do work?

MANY souls find it very difficult to accept their loving relationship with all human beings. This separation is the cause of all the trouble in the world, the cause of all strife and wars. The place to start putting things right is in yourself and your own personal relationships with all those souls with whom you come into contact. Cease pointing your finger and being critical of those souls with whom you cannot get along in the world. Put your own house in order. You have more than enough to cope with yourself, without tearing your fellow human beings to pieces and pointing out all their faults and failings and where they have gone wrong. When you are willing to face yourself and put things right within, then you will be able to help your fellow human beings simply by your example, not by criticism, intolerance and many words. Love your fellow human beings as I love you. Help them, bless them, encourage them and see the very best in them.

*K*NOW with an inner certainty that I never give you more to carry than you are capable of, and that you never have to carry it alone, for I AM with you always. Therefore let us do everything together. When you are truly aware of this support, you will never again feel overburdened by the weight of your responsibilities, no matter how great they may be. I need those souls who are willing to shoulder responsibilities and do not shy away from them, for I have to work in and through dedicated souls who are willing to forget the self completely in service to Me and to their fellow human beings. Are you willing to do it? This life calls for complete dedication and consistency. Are you consistent in your work for Me? Do you dedicate each day to My service? Are you obedient to My slightest whisper? Surely by now you realise that all things work together for good only when you truly love Me and put Me first in everything.

ET there be balance in everything. Work hard but also learn to play hard, and do what you love doing, whatever it may be. It matters not whether your pleasures are simple or extravagant, as long as you find a real joy in them. When you are doing something you enjoy, it matters not how strenuous it may be; you will not feel exhausted but exhilarated and uplifted. Work should never be a drudgery, and it never will be when your attitude towards it is right and you enjoy what you are doing. When you have balance in your life, you will find a wholeness in life, and you will not have an overdose of either work or play. One is as bad as the other. Never compare your pleasures with anyone else's; what you enjoy doing may not appeal to anyone else. Do what you enjoy doing and let the others follow what appeals to them. Live and let live.

ALWAYS remember, when you long for something badly enough, you can bring it about. When you long for oneness, for wholeness, it can be yours if you go all out to bring it about. Your love and longing to be at one with Me will follow as day follows night, and nothing can stop it. It is something that takes place deep within every soul, and once that seed of longing has been planted, it will grow and grow. What is your deepest longing? Do you want to give all to Me? Are you willing to give up all those little self-indulgences and desires which can cause separation? It is up to you to make your own decision and know your heart's desire. Do not expect anyone else to tell you what it is. It is something you must do yourself without any outer help. I AM here to help you. Seek My help at all times.

IFE is full and overflowing with the new, but it is necessary to empty out the old to make room for the new to enter. The emptying out process can be very painful, for when you have been emptied of the old, you may experience that feeling of having nothing to hold on to and of being alone and bereft of everything. You may feel that life is completely dead and empty with no meaning to it, and you want to throw up your hands in despair. Realise that if you are going through such a time, it is this process of being emptied of the old so that you can be refilled with the new. Never give up hope, but hold on until you are completely empty and drained of everything. Then you can start again in newness of Spirit and in truth. You can become as a little child and enjoy to the full the wonderment of this new life as you gradually become infilled by it.

I AM love. To know Me, you must have love in your heart; for without love you cannot know Me. Keep the love flowing freely and learn to love what you are doing; love your environment and love all those souls around you. Love and never count the cost; never seek for reward. You can never give too much love, so do not be afraid and try to withdraw the love flow, even when you are rebuffed. When this happens, it is easy to close up your heart and withdraw for fear of being hurt. Do not do it; it will only make you hard and brittle, and in that state you will never be able to help another soul, for no one is drawn to someone with a hard, unloving heart. Use wisdom and understanding in conjunction with love, and in this way you will keep the perfect balance. The primary lesson of life is to learn to love. Waste no time and learn that lesson quickly.

I S your life running smoothly? Are you content with what you are doing? Do you feel at peace with the world, or is your life full of ups and downs? Are you dissatisfied with the way you are living or with the work you are doing? Do you find it difficult to harmonise with those souls around you? Do you blame your discontent and dissatisfaction on those people with whom you are in contact and on your circumstances and situation? Do you feel that if you were somewhere else all would be well and you would be at peace? When you are at perfect peace deep within, it does not matter where you are, or whom you are with, or what very ordinary, mundane job you are doing. Nothing will be able to disturb you or throw you off balance, because you are perfectly balanced and in harmony within. Instead of fighting against your circumstances, learn to flow with them and so find that inner peace and understanding deep within.

I AM the source of all life. When you get into rhythm with Me, everything flows smoothly. Many souls wonder why life is full of ups and downs or why many things go wrong and immediately they are ready to blame everything and everybody but themselves. When you take time to find out why you are out of harmony with life, you will very often find that you are not putting first things first and that you are failing to take time to go into the silence and find out in the peace and stillness what I require of you. It takes time, it takes patience, it takes faith and belief. It means you have to learn to be still. I want you to learn to work out the answers to your problems alone with Me. I long for you to rely on Me entirely for everything, to realise that your strength, your wisdom, your understanding all come from Me.

WHEN you feel you have reached the end and you cannot go one step further, or when life seems to be drained of all purpose, what a wonderful opportunity to start all over again! It is something all souls can do if they want to and if they can accept, in true humility, that they only make a mess of their lives when they try to handle them on their own. They can do it if they are willing to hand their lives over to Me and let Me run them. Give constant thanks for this new day and for a new way, for a new opportunity to start again. Realise that I have need of you, and when you are in a negative state, you shut yourself off from Me. Call upon Me and I will answer you. I will be with you in trouble. I will uplift you and set your feet upon the right path and will guide your every step. I AM with you always.

MY plan for you is perfect and will fall into place at exactly the right time. Never try to hurry anything along, but watch everything unfold and develop. If life appears to be going very slowly, be not impatient. Learn to wait upon Me in absolute faith and confidence, and know that at the right time all things will come about, as there is indeed a right time and a right season for everything. Remember, you cannot change the seasons of the year; you cannot change the movement of the heavens or the tides. The universe is in My hands and no one can harm it. Go forward in complete faith and confidence, allowing My wonders and glories to unfold. Be afraid of nothing, but be strong and of good courage. When you are at perfect peace within, you will be able to withstand the stresses and strains without. Therefore let My peace and love infil and enfold you, and be at perfect peace as you do My will.

WASTE no time in idle thoughts and chatter. Use every moment of time in loving, positive, constructive thoughts and words. Realise that the thoughts you project can help or mar; therefore be master of your thoughts and words and not a slave to them. Why not enjoy life to the full? You can only do that when you are giving of your very best in time, words and deeds. Open your eyes and open your heart and see and feel the very best in everything and everyone around you. If you have difficulty in finding the very best, simply keep on looking for it until you have found it; it is there waiting for you. There are many wonderful things in the world. Why not take time to concentrate on them and fill your life with them, so that the unpleasant, unhappy and discordant ones can find no place in your life? Life is what you make it. What are you making of yours?

*Y*OU cannot play a game of tennis just by standing there with a racquet and ball in your hand. You have to raise the racquet and hit the ball over the net. You have to take action. So with faith. You have to do something to prove to yourself that it does work when you live by it. The more you try it and realise that it works, the more confident you become until you are willing to take any step in faith without hesitation because you know we are taking it together, and anything is possible when you are willing to do so. You have to have faith in your ability to swim before you jump into deep water with complete confidence; otherwise you will drown. You have to have faith in the ability to live by faith before you can do it. Faith begets faith. How can you tell whether you can trust Me unless you try it and see if it is so?

HESE are crucial times and each soul is needed in its rightful place. It is like a vast jigsaw puzzle being put together: there is a right place for every tiny piece. Are you in your rightful place? Only you will know. Do you feel you blend in perfectly with the whole and that you do not create any jarring or discordant note? Peace, harmony and tranquillity must be within you to stabilise you and bring you into alignment with what is about to take place. Therefore it is necessary to be still and find that peace within so that nothing and no one can disturb it. Be like an anchor, strong and steady, so that no storm without can affect you or shift you from your rightful place. Hold fast and know that all is very, very well and that all is proceeding according to My perfect plan. Let not your heart be troubled, but put your whole trust, faith and security in Me.

*A*S you learn to give, so will you receive. Open your heart and give all you can of the gifts which have been given you. Give of your love, your wisdom, your understanding. Give of the intangible as well as the tangible. In fact, give and give and go on giving without any thought of the self, without any thought of the cost or what you will get out of it. Your giving must be whole-hearted and joyous; then you will find the very act of giving will bring with it joy and happiness untold. Every soul has something to give, so find out what you have to give and then give it. Never forget there are many levels on which you can give. Do not just give what is easy to give, but give where it hurts, and grow and expand as you do so, for only the very best can come out of your giving.

RELAX and know that there is time for everything. Everyone has an equal amount of time, but it is how you use it that matters. Do you use it to the full and enjoy every moment of it, or do you dissipate time by failing to put first things first? Cease being a slave to time. Why not make it your servant instead? Then it will never rule you but you will rule it. Accept that you can only do one thing at a time, do it perfectly and then move on to the next. Never try to look too far ahead. You can only live one moment at a time. If you try and plan too far ahead, you may be very disappointed when things do not work out as you had planned. Many changes can take place and in your planning you cannot account for them. It is best to live fully in the moment and let the future take care of itself.

NEVER waste time and energy wishing you were somewhere else, doing something else. Accept your situation and realise you are where you are, doing what you are doing, for a very specific reason. Realise that nothing is by chance, that you have certain lessons to learn and that the situation you are in has been given to you to enable you to learn those lessons as quickly as possible, so that you can move onward and upward along this spiritual path. Surely you do not want to get stuck in a rut, no matter how safe and secure that rut may appear to be! Think how dull and uninteresting life would be if a rut were your choice. Life is full of excitement and expectancy when you are willing to move ahead fearlessly into the unknown and take the next step in absolute faith and confidence with Me as your guide and companion. Fear not; I AM with you always.

*A*LWAYS remember that you can do something about the state of the world by a complete change of heart, mind and spirit. It is when you realise it, shoulder your responsibilities and do something about it that changes will come about, in small ways to begin with and then spreading out until all is included. Consider how wonderful it is, how encouraging, to know that you can do something to rectify the state of the world by changing within, and so reflect those changes without. Blessed are they who are willing and open and see the need for change and do something about it; for they are like the yeast in the lump of dough that enables the bread to rise. Without the yeast the bread would not rise. Without change all would remain static, become stagnant and die. So change and expand in real joy and thanksgiving, and be grateful that you can do it; and get into action now.

MANY times you have heard the words, 'Life is what you make it,' but what have you done about it? Do you not realise that you control your life, your happiness, your success, your joys and your sorrows? Life can be wonderful, thrilling and glorious, but it is up to you to make it so by expecting the very best. Live one day at a time and live it to the full. Never waste time worrying about tomorrow and what it may bring, or allow yourself to become depressed because you feel you cannot cope with whatever that may be. Always look on the bright side of life and concentrate on it in the ever-present now. Because yesterday did not go smoothly does not mean that today will be the same. Leave yesterday behind; learn from it, but do not allow it to spoil today. Today lies in front of you, untouched and unblemished. What are you going to do with it?

I T is important in life to have a goal and to keep moving towards it. See a real purpose and plan in your life, though you may not always be able to see the goal clearly; for when you go down into a valley or the way is twisty, you cannot always see around the next corner. You will find that every now and again you will be given an uplifting spiritual experience which will carry you through the rough places and will enable you to keep on, no matter what you are faced with. Aim high—the higher the better. Then you will have to keep moving, growing and expanding to get there. You can never sit back and be self-satisfied; you can never remain static. You are always reaching for that next rung on the ladder of life, and you know that every rung takes you nearer the goal, no matter how far away it may be. So keep on and on, and never give up.

I was shown autumn leaves falling from a tree and then a tree stripped of every leaf. I heard the words:

Be not concerned. The life force is within and from that life force the new shall spring forth. Know that the old must die so that the new can be born.

EARN to be a real optimist and expect the very best in everything you undertake. Know that you can and will do it perfectly and that there will be nothing slap-dash in your work or in your life. Simply do it unto Me and to My glory and you are bound to do everything with love, and therefore in true perfection. This principle also applies to the way you look and the way you behave. When you are doing everything for Me and when your greatest desire is to do My will because of your love for me, you will always want to do everything well. You will always want to look your best and give of your best, and you will never be satisfied with anything less. It is necessary every now and again to take time and see where you need to change, and then be willing to do so. Learn to change and change quickly, and know that every change is indeed for the very best.

VERY soul has something to share. There are gifts and possessions on many different levels. You may not have material gifts but you may be sure you have other gifts, whatever they are. Hold them not to the self but be willing to bring them out into the open, uncover them and then use them as they should be used, never for the glorification of the self but always to My honour and glory. Possess nothing, but use and enjoy all you have to the full. What have you to give? Take time to find out, if you do not know. Give whole-heartedly and give with joy, and be grateful that you have something to give, whatever it may be. When you have chosen to live this way of life completely dedicated to Me and to My work, you can no longer cling onto anything. Realise that all you have is Mine, and therefore it is there to be shared with the whole.

YOU hold a great responsibility in your hands, for I pour down upon you all My good and perfect gifts. Your feet have been set on the path leading to the New Age, and all the time you are moving further and further into it and becoming part of it. You can no longer make excuses for yourself when you fail to do what you should be doing, by saying you did not know or did not realise, for you are responsible for your every action. You know how to control your thoughts and your actions; therefore do so. Never try to hide behind ignorance, but know that within you you contain all knowledge, all wisdom, all understanding; and it is simply a question of drawing from that limitless supply at all times. Give eternal thanks that you do know the truth and that it is the truth that enables you to do what is required of you. Be at perfect peace.

HOW can you expect to live a deep spiritual life unless you are willing to make an effort to do something about it? You cannot live on other souls' experiences, glories and triumphs, on other souls' oneness with Me. It is something you have to seek and find for yourself. Start right now doing your own thinking and standing on your own feet, and cease leaning on anyone else. When a person has been on crutches for some time, unless they are willing to throw aside those crutches and make the effort to walk without them, they will go through life depending on them and lose the use of their legs altogether. That is why it is vitally important for you to stand on your own feet spiritually and receive your inspiration from within and not from without. Each one will receive it in a different way. There is no set pattern. Find out your way and start living it now.

WHAT are you doing with your life? Are you content to drift through life, doing what you want to, living the way you want to live, without a thought for anyone else? You are free to do it. Many, many souls live this way and then wonder why they are unhappy and discontented. It is only when you learn to forget the self and live for others that you will find real peace of heart and true contentment. I AM here to show you the way, but you have to take it. No one else can take it for you; no one else can live your life for you. Learn to give and not just take all the time. Why not give on one level and receive on another? Life is a two-way thing, a constant giving and receiving. You cannot live unto yourself and find real happiness and satisfaction in life. Live for the whole and give to the whole and be whole.

*Y*OU can make this day whatever you want it to be. The very moment you wake up in the morning you can decide what sort of day it is going to be for you. It can be the most wonderful and inspiring day imaginable, but it is up to you. You are free to make the choice. So why not start by giving thanks to open your heart? The more thankful you are, the more open you are to all the wonderful happenings this day can bring. Love, praise and gratitude fling open wide the portals and allow the light to stream in and reveal all the very best in life. Be determined to be ultra-positive today, to expect the very best and draw it to you. Have absolute faith and confidence that you can and will do it. Let there be no doubts in your ability to do it. Simply know that with Me all things are possible and that you are doing everything with Me.

D O you long to do My will, or are you still afraid that the cost may be too great? Remember, I do ask for everything; therefore there can be no holding back anything. It is only when all is given—and given freely and with love—that all shall be returned to you. Does the sacrifice seem too great to you? When something is given in love, there is no question of its being a sacrifice, but rather a real delight, joy and pleasure. Why hesitate? When all is given freely and you possess nothing, then everything is yours. You have nothing to lose and everything to gain, and the whole world is at your feet. You know that all you have comes from Me, the source of all, and that all is there to be drawn on as the need arises. Therefore you can draw from My storehouse of abundant riches which are limitless and are here for all those souls who love Me and put Me first in everything.

*L*ET your eye be single, and see yourself whole, perfect and made in My image and likeness. Never belittle yourself or think the worst of yourself. Raise your thinking and be very positive about yourself. If you have made mistakes, learn to forgive yourself and then move forward and upward. I have no need for you to scourge yourself and to go about full of self-concern and self-pity. Do you not realise that when you do so, you shut yourself off from Me and I cannot use you? Keep open; learn from your mistakes. Forget the self completely in love and service to your·fellow human beings. As soon as you start thinking of others, the self is forgotten. Service is a great healer, a great renewer of balance and stability. So find out what your very best is, what you are good at; and when you know what it is, then go ahead and give it with your whole heart. Keep moving forward, never backward.

EVERY soul longs for the very best in life. The very best is there waiting for you when you are ready to accept it. But you must be willing to accept it wholeheartedly with real joy and without any feeling of being unworthy or not being ready for it. If that is your attitude, you block that which is your true heritage, and it cannot flow to you. Therefore see that there is nothing in you which is holding it up. I AM holding out life, life more abundant. I AM holding out beauty, harmony, peace, love. The ways of the Spirit are yours. Walk in those ways, live in perfect harmony with My laws and watch everything fall into place in true perfection. Let there be no stress or strain in you. Simply accept that which is yours with a full and grateful heart, and never forget to express your love and appreciation for all that is being poured down upon you.

WHAT is deep within you is reflected without. When there is order, harmony, beauty and peace within, it will be reflected in everything you do, say and think. Whereas if there is confusion, disorder and disharmony within, it cannot be hidden but will be reflected in your whole life and living. When change comes, it has to start from within and work out. Then it will be lasting, and nothing will be able to throw it off balance. Do not sit back and expect your life to change, but get into action and do something about it. You can start right now by working on your own inner state. You do not have to wait for anyone else to change; you can do your own changing without any further delay. Give constant thanks that you are able to do something about it without any hold-ups. If there are any hold-ups, they are within yourself; therefore you are the one who can do something about them.

THE fruit of the Spirit is joy, so let there be more joy in your life and more fun and laughter. It is so important that there is balance and moderation in all things so that life can be enjoyed to the full. You may enjoy the work you are doing and feel you do not need a change. Every now and again you need to break away and do something entirely different to change the rhythm of your life. You will find when you do, you will be able to go back to the work which has to be done completely refreshed, and you will be able to do it with new zest and enjoyment. Life should never be a burden. You are not here to be bowed down by the weight of the world. You are here to make the very most of life and enjoy every moment of it, because you are living a balanced life, and there is a constant giving and receiving.

CAN you truly love when you are beset by tests and trials, and you feel everything and everyone is against you? It is easy enough to love when everything is going smoothly. It is when you find yourself up against it that you are inclined to close your heart and stop the flow of love; and yet it is the time when the need for love is even greater. When you can love despite all outer conditions, then you can be sure it is My divine love which is flowing in and through you, and that this wondrous love will win through in the end. Love never gives up; it will try one way and then another until it wins through. Love is gentle, and yet strong and persistent. Like water it wears a way through to the very hardest of hearts. So never accept 'no' for an answer. Love and keep on loving, and watch the way open up.

*G*IVE eternal thanks for all My good and perfect gifts which I pour down upon you. Realise you always have all that you need whenever you have need of it. I know all your needs before you even ask for them. You are a steward of all I bestow upon you; therefore be a good steward. Never try to possess anything, but use all you have with great wisdom and understanding. You came into this world with nothing, and you will go out of it with nothing. All you have I have given to you to use to the full while you are on this earth plane. Why not enjoy everything and give thanks for it all, but do not try to hold on to it. Freely has it been given to you; freely give it to those souls around you. Share all you have, and so make room for more and more to be drawn to you. Know that your every need is wonderfully met as you live by My laws.

DEPENDABILITY is the heart of responsibility. It means you are always at the right place at the right time doing what you know has to be done. You never put off until tomorrow what you know you must do today. When you put your hand to something, you will see it through, no matter what opposition you come up against. You are never discouraged by obstacles, but see them as stepping stones and as challenges to be overcome. You are as steady as a rock because your security and stability are within, and you are not affected by outer conditions and chaos and confusion all around you. Whatever happens, you are not up one day and down the next. That is what it means to be absolutely reliable and dependable; that is being strong and of good courage. As you shoulder more and more responsibilities dependably, you will become stronger and stronger, until nothing is too much for you.

IVE and work, but do not forget to play, to have fun in life and enjoy it. You need balance in everything. Too much work and no play makes life lopsided, and makes you dull and uninteresting. Seek perfect balance in everything you do, and you will find life a real joy. You need variety in life, so why not break out and attempt something quite new and different, not because you are bored with what you are doing or because you want to run away from it, but because you realise you need a change? When you can do it without any sense of guilt, you will find you will be able to do all you have to do with a new outlook; and, what is more, you will be able to do it with real enjoyment. What is the use of life unless you can enjoy it and have a good time in everything you undertake, whether you call it work or play?

ET your love and compassion be extended to all; not just to those souls who love you, but even to those souls who hate you and who despitefully use you. As you raise your consciousness and remain in a raised state, you will be able to see everything from a different perspective and will see that you have no enemies. So do not harden your heart and want to retaliate when life seems to be going against you. Simply know and accept that I AM with you, that I AM guiding and directing you, and that all is very, very well. Then let go and see only the very best come out of every situation. It is when you are willing to do it that you are able to see My wonders and glories come about and know without a shadow of doubt that on your own strength you would not be able to accomplish such wonders. Therefore lift up your heart and give Me the honour and glory.

ALL things are part of the perfect whole; and everything you do, say, think and feel is part of it. Therefore do not limit yourself in any way but feel yourself expand and expand, taking in more and more. You will never reach the limits because there is no limit. Life is infinite and you are part of that infinity. Keep stretching your consciousness. Where is that spirit of adventure within you that enables you to step out fearlessly into the unknown with a feeling of real excitement and expectation? Simply going along in the same old way day in and day out will get you nowhere, and you cannot hope to grow spiritually. You have to want to move forward, and when you make your own decision to do so, then you will receive help from every side. The first move is always yours. So do not waste time hanging back, but take the first step forward and behold miracle upon miracle taking place in your life.

I AM your refuge and strength, a very present help in times of distress and trouble. Learn to call upon Me, to lean upon Me, to draw from Me, to put your whole faith and trust in Me, and as you do so see every difficulty and problem dissolve into nothingness. There is the perfect answer to every problem. Look for it and you will find it. Waste no time wallowing in your problems and in self-pity, but rise above them. Give thanks that the answer is right there when you expand your consciousness and have faith that the answer is there waiting to be put into action when you can still your mind. 'Be ye transformed by the renewing of your mind.' You can solve every problem simply by knowing that the answer is there when you can become still and take time to seek and find it. Cease running round in circles, getting nowhere. Call upon Me.

IF you have lost your way, the quickest and easiest method of finding it again is to become still, and in the peace and stillness seek your direction. Are you willing to take time to be still and to seek within, or do you feel it is a waste of time and you must get on and do all that has to be done? Every soul needs direction, for without it you may indeed become completely lost in the maze of life. So why not spend a short time each day alone with Me to determine where you are going? As you learn to do it, you will find the deep inner need for this communion and will long to spend more and more time with Me in this state of consciousness. Therefore keep alert and answer those deep yearnings within you; never push them aside impatiently, feeling there is no time. I tell you there is time for everything.

ARE you not part of the whole? Then why separate yourself by living a disordered, chaotic life? As you fill your mind with beautiful thoughts, say beautiful words and accomplish beautiful things, so do you become one with the beautiful wholeness which is My universe, and everything fits in perfectly. As each individual seeks and finds that inner peace and harmony, so will peace and harmony reign in the world. It has to start somewhere, so why not let it start in you? Realise that you, by doing your part, can help to bring peace and harmony into the world. It is every tiny drop of water that makes up the mighty ocean and every tiny grain of sand that makes up the beach. Therefore every individual at peace within can bring outer peace into the world. So why not do your part now? Lift up your heart and give eternal thanks that you know you have a part to play, and go ahead and play it.

EXPAND your consciousness and know I AM all there is. Then go on and on expanding it, and see the all-inclusiveness of the I AM. Feel yourself growing, breaking all bonds which have held you and have stifled your growth and expansion. Just as a tiny seed planted in the earth breaks its outer skin and begins to expand and develop into that which it really is, so let your real self grow and expand until you become what you really are, and behold the wonder of it all. As you do so, know that you are one with all life, now and forever, that never again can you be separated from it, and that I AM in you and you are in the I AM. You will be able to do all things and know that absolutely nothing is impossible, for it is the I AM who is working in and through you. When I AM recognised and accepted, anything is possible.

TOP for a moment in all your busyness, and see what you are putting first. Is it work? Is it living? Is it your wants? Your desires? Seek ye first My kingdom. Find your direct contact with Me and all else shall be added unto you. Do you not realise that your communion with Me means far more than anything else, for it is from this contact that all else stems. Do your part and put first things first. You cannot draw water from a well unless you get a bucket and let it down into the well, fill it with water and then draw it up. You have to do something; you have to make the effort and do your part. Standing at the top of the well looking at the water will not draw it up. So with this spiritual life: standing around watching others find their oneness with Me will not do it for you. Every soul has to do its own inner seeking and finding.

IF you find yourself in a situation which is hard to accept and love, there is always something you can do about it if you want to; for as you go into the silence and seek Me, I will throw the light of truth on the situation. I will reveal to you why you are where you are, and why you are doing what you are doing. You may be sure there is a very good reason for it and that there are vitally important lessons to be learnt. Until you change your attitude and learn to love where you are, who you are with and what you are doing, you will have to remain in that situation. As soon as those lessons have been learnt and you truly love what you are doing and do it whole-heartedly for Me and for My sake, then you will move on to something else. Watch love open all doors for you.

BECAUSE something was right and proper yesterday does not mean it is today. That is why you have to live one day at a time, and live fully in the ever-present, glorious now; for when you can do it without any reservations and preconceived ideas, you will be able to accept change without resistance and life will flow with ease and smoothness. It is much easier to say it than to do it, especially when you have felt everything was going smoothly and have sunk your roots down deep, feeling secure in your present situation. Let your security be in Me and never in a situation, a plan, a person or a thing; for what is here today may be gone tomorrow. But I AM always here through all eternity. Therefore seek Me and find Me, and fear nothing. Let the changes come, and simply know that each change will be for the very best and that each one is necessary for the growth and expansion of the whole.

*T*HE higher your aims and goals, the better. Never limit yourself in any way. Simply know that you can accomplish anything that you set out to do because you are drawing your help and strength from Me, and there is no such thing as defeat or failure. Whatever has My hallmark on it is bound to succeed, and only the highest results can come from it. Therefore keep your consciousness raised, get into tune with all life and behold the most wonderful results. You cannot expect these results unless you are in rhythm with the highest good within you, can flow freely with all that is going on and move through all that would hold you up. There are many things in life that would block you from reaching your goal. Sweep them all aside and refuse to contemplate failure for even one second. Simply know you can and will succeed, and success will be yours in everything you undertake.

*T*HERE is not one way which is right and all the rest wrong. Mountain climbers have to make the choice between climbing straight up to the summit by the direct route, or finding an easier route to follow. It is up to them. You make up your mind which is the right spiritual path for you and then follow it whole-heartedly. There are those souls who are seekers and have not yet found their specific path in this life. They will try one spiritual path after another and follow it a certain distance, then realise it is not for them and start off on another path. They will keep on doing it until they have found the right one. They will find the right one if they seek diligently and never give up their search. If you have found your rightful path, move ever forward and waste no time looking back or being critical of those souls who are still searching.

A new concept is like a seed planted in the warmth of your house. The seed cannot be taken straight out of that atmosphere until it is strong enough to be planted where it has to withstand the outer elements. So with a new concept: it cannot be pulled out like a conjuror pulls a rabbit out of a hat. It takes time to give it substance and form. It has to be tried out with the few before it can be given to the many. It takes great love and patience to do it; it takes dedication and devotion. This process is what is taking place at this time with the New Age. It is very new. Many new ideas and concepts are being born, and each one has to be tried out, understood, loved and cherished. When you are at the spearhead of the New Age, you must be willing to go ahead fearlessly and try out the newest of the new.

EVERYTHING improves with practice. The more you learn to live a life, the more it becomes a part of you, and you can live and move and have your being in it. You cannot remain static, so let yourself grow and expand freely and joyously. Break those bonds which have kept you confined in the past. Rise above all those fears which have prevented you from expanding and have kept you blindfolded, so that you have been unable to see clearly the glorious vision before you. Demonstrate what faith means to you and expect the seemingly impossible to become possible. Bring My kingdom down on earth, and learn to do My will and walk in My ways. No matter how weak and faltering those first steps may be, they have to be taken. It does not matter how many times you fall. Simply pick yourself up and try again and again.

*A*LWAYS seek the best, always expect the best and never at any time be content with second best. It may be difficult for you, especially at times when you think you are scraping the bottom of the barrel. Then you have to raise your consciousness, and never for one second think lack, but think abundance. See abundance and give thanks for My infinite and limitless supply. Why are you content to accept second best, when the very best is waiting for you to accept it, waiting to bless you? When you can think big, your whole life and living will expand within and around you. Remember, it all starts from within and it all starts with you. Start right now to readjust your thinking. Become reoriented from within, and let it gradually work from within like yeast in a lump of dough. Never fail to recognise My hand in everything, and give constant thanks. Take nothing for granted, but realise how blessed you are.

EARN to give freely of all that you have. Learn also to receive graciously all that is given to you, and use it wisely for the expansion and betterment of the whole. When you give, give freely and do not count the cost. That which is given in the right spirit, whole-heartedly and in purest love, will bring great joy and blessings to the many and will multiply and grow. Always remember, let there be no strings attached to what you give. Give and then forget about it. When you do a job, do it with love, and be grateful that you have the gift and ability to do it. Do it perfectly, and never do it for what you can get out of it. When you can learn to do everything to My honour and glory, then you will have learnt the art of true giving. You will find the greatest joy in everything you give, and your whole attitude and outlook will be right.

HERE is more to faith than sitting back and leaving everything to Me. You have your part to play, for 'according to your faith, be it unto you'. When your complete faith and trust are in Me, then anything is possible. Live by faith and demonstrate My laws for all souls to see. Let us work as one, live as one, be as one; I in you and you in Me. When you fully understand that I can do anything, then you realise that you can do anything, for I AM working in and through you. Nothing will get done unless you take the action and do it. I AM within you and you are My hands and feet. Dedicate those hands and feet to Me and to My service, so that there is nothing to hold up the work and everything runs smoothly. See that you work in perfect harmony and rhythm with My laws, and behold wonder upon wonder come about; and give eternal thanks for everything.

I was shown the earth like a draught board painted in big black and white squares. As rain came down, the black paint ran into the white, and the whole became a dirty grey. Then even heavier rain came, and the whole was transformed into purest white. I heard the words:

Have faith. Hold fast and know that the whole earth and all in it are going through a tremendous cleansing process. All is very, very well, for all is going according to My plan. Be at perfect peace.

HERE is no strain or stress in nature. A seed goes through its full cycle; it does not have to do anything; it just has to allow it all to happen. All you have to do is to allow it all to happen. Why not let yourself be transformed into a glorious butterfly? Come out of that chrysalis, that confined space, out of the restrictions of your mortal mind and ideas. When a snake changes its skin, it slowly wriggles out of its old one and leaves it behind to wither away and disintegrate. A crab outgrows its shell as it grows and expands, and grows a bigger, more beautiful one. A bird cracks open its shell and emerges completely transformed. It is free, free, free! That is what is waiting to happen to you. A new freedom, a new joy, a whole new world is waiting to open up for you when you are willing to move out of those old restrictive ways, thoughts and ideas, and be transformed.

HEN you are first taught to do anything, whether it is driving a car, learning to swim or learning to play a musical instrument, you are very aware of every movement, every action you make. You make mistakes but you never give up. You rectify those mistakes and keep on trying until you have mastered whatever it is. Then you find you no longer have to think of every movement; you do it automatically; you flow with it and enjoy it because it is no longer an effort. So it is with this spiritual life. As it becomes a part of you, you no longer have to be reminded to be consciously aware of Me and of My divine presence, because you are aware of it. You no longer have to get into tune with Me because you are in tune. It is all as natural to you as breathing. In this state you know that I AM in you, and you are in Me, and we are one.

ENTER this day with your heart overflowing with love, joy and thanksgiving, overjoyed to be alive, to be doing what you are doing, to be where you are; and see the perfection of this day emerge. Blessed are those souls who can see the beauty, joy and harmony all around them and appreciate it to the full, and those souls who recognise Me in everything and everyone and give thanks for all. Joy is like a stone thrown into the middle of a pool of water; the ripples go out and out to the far edges of the pool and then return to the centre, bringing joy to all they contact on the way. Love is like a healing balm, healing all wounds, all hurts, all sorrows; so love with My divine love; love the lovable and the seeming unlovable; love those souls who know not the meaning of love; love your so-called enemies. When your heart is filled with love, you will know no enemies. Love is the foundation of this spiritual life.

*K*EEP your eyes open and keep ever alert. Behold My hand in everything and give eternal thanks. Without awareness you can miss so much which is right there in front of you, or even within you. Many souls go through life blind to the wonders all around them, blind to the miracles of nature, and so miss the miracles of life. When you are aware of beauty, harmony, peace and serenity in the small things around you, you will find that awareness growing until all life becomes a wonderland and you walk through life like a child, wide-eyed at all that is taking place. You will expect the most glorious happenings to take place, and therefore will help to bring them about. There will never be a dull moment in your life. You will take nothing for granted, but will give thanks for everything. Gratitude keeps the door wide open for more and more wonders to enter your life, so never, never fail to give thanks.

ACCEPT your oneness with all life; accept your oneness with Me. Do not shy away from it, feeling you are not worthy to accept our oneness. This feeling of unworthiness is what separates individuals from Me, their creator. For too long, people have been told they are miserable sinners and are not worthy to walk and talk with Me. For too long they have separated themselves from Me, until they no longer know Me, no longer realise that I AM within them. Banish forever all these false concepts of Me. I AM love. I AM within you. Accept with joy and wonderment our oneness. Accept it as a very small child, and do not waste time and energy trying to work it out with your mind. If you try to approach this life intellectually, you waste much time and fail to see the simplicity of it. My ways are simple; cease making them complicated for yourself.

THESE are no ordinary times. Behold the unfolding of My vast and glorious plan. Now is the time for the most wonderful changes to come about, so be prepared for anything at any time. There is nothing casual or by chance about those souls who are being drawn together at this time for the tremendous work ahead. There is a very definite plan unfolding; unfold with it. Do not be anxious about anything; banish all fear. Recognise My hand in everything, see the perfection of it all and give eternal thanks for it. Be ready and willing to accept your responsibilities. This life is not for the shirkers or those souls who are afraid of responsibilities. The New Age demands strength, courage and dedication, as well as rock-like faith and belief. It is a wonderful adventure, and therefore the spirit of adventure is required to move right into it and become part of it. Move with all that is happening, quietly and peacefully, without any strain, for all is very, very well.

HAVE you found what you can contribute to the whole? Can you feel yourself blending in, or do you feel you are standing on the outside looking in, wondering where your place is? Why not step right in, and by doing so find that special place more quickly? Once you feel you are part of that whole, you will want to give of your very best. I liken this process to a clock with all its many parts. Every part is needed for the clock to keep the right time. It is when each part is in its rightful place doing its specific job that precision timing is achieved. Every soul longs to be wanted, to be needed. When you feel needed, you begin to grow, flower and flourish and give of your very best. Always remember that I have need of you. Offer yourself anew to Me each day so that I can use you as I will, and grow in strength and stature.

WHY accept any limitations anywhere in your life? Feel yourself expanding in consciousness day by day. Expect the new to unfold within you and before you, and if it calls for changes in you, be willing to change without hesitation. When you want to change a programme on the radio, you have to turn the knob until you find the new station. Then you have to take great care to tune in until the reception is clear and there are no distortions to spoil the programme. When your desire to move out of the old is great enough, you will leave no stone unturned until you have done so. You will turn every knob until you are tuned in to the new and can receive it loudly and clearly. With this clear reception you then have to be still and listen; and when you have absorbed what is being transmitted, you then have to get into action and do something about it. Why wait another day? Tune in now.

LET your faith be strong and unshakable. Faith has to be lived and demonstrated, not talked about. It grows stronger and stronger when used constantly. It is not something to be taken from a shelf every now and again, used and then put back again until it is next needed. As you learn to live by faith, you will learn to see Me in everyone and everything that is taking place, and realise that there is nowhere where I AM not. It is an inner awareness that all the very best of life stems from within. When you realise that you contain all within you, you will cease that eternal search. You will cease striving and struggling to reach the impossible, and in quietness and confidence find that storehouse full to overflowing of untold treasures. Now is the time to live by faith, not tomorrow or one day when you are feeling stronger and have more confidence. Put it into practice right now and see how wonderfully it works.

DAY by day you are aware of new developments within and without you. You find yourself absorbing new ideas and new ways. Your consciousness expands and is able to accept more and more. Some people learn more quickly than others; therefore moving into the New Age will not be the same for everyone. Some souls will be able to leap into it. Some souls will move slowly into it, testing every step of the way. Some souls will crawl into it and find every step painful because they are resisting the changes which are taking place. They resent those new ways and new ideas and long to be left alone to live in the same old way, with the attitude that what was good enough for their fathers and mothers is good enough for them. The answer to that attitude is to stop fighting against it and to get into tune and flow with life. Times are changing and changing fast, and unless you change with them, you will be left behind.

ALL that you need you have within you, waiting to be recognised, developed and drawn forth. An acorn contains within it a mighty oak. You contain within you tremendous potential. Just as the acorn has to be planted and tended to enable it to grow and become that mighty oak, so that which is within you has to be recognised before it can be drawn forth and used to the full; otherwise it lives dormant within you. What happens to many souls is that this tremendous potential never develops in this life and is often carried over from one life to another. How unnecessary this process is! Now is the time to draw forth and use all that you have within you. Know that you can do all things because I AM there strengthening and guiding your every movement and decision, until like that acorn you have burst your bonds and are free to grow into the mighty oak.

EVER waste time feeling you have a very long way to go in this spiritual life. Instead, be encouraged and strengthened by realising how far you have come, and give eternal thanks for it. Realise how much you have to be grateful for. Surround yourself with beautiful thoughts, with beautiful things, with beautiful people. See the light of truth shining in everything and everyone. Let your light shine brightly from deep within you. Know that nothing without can extinguish it and that only your negativity can do it. Therefore keep positive all the time. Always choose the path of light and ignore the darkness, thereby giving it no strength. More and more light is needed as the hunger for spiritual food grows greater in the world, so keep your light burning brightly. Be light and let it shine forth from you, pushing back the darkness. Be love and let love flow from you freely, and help meet the tremendous need in the world.

AS you expect the very best in life, you draw it to you; so start right now expecting the very best in everything and everyone, and watch the very best come about. Expect your every need to be met. Expect the answer to every problem. Expect abundance on every level. Expect to grow spiritually. Accept no limitations in your life; simply know and accept that all My good and perfect gifts are yours as you learn to get your values right and put first things first in your life. Expect to grow in stature and beauty, in wisdom and understanding. Expect to be used as a channel for My divine love and light to flow in and through. Accept that I can use you for My work. Do it all in absolute faith and confidence, and behold My wonders and glories come about, not just once in a while but all the time, so that your whole life is indeed a song of joy and thanksgiving.

HOW many times have I told you I need you free to do all that has to be done? When will you learn to let go and be free? You will never know the meaning of freedom until you are willing to let go, have confidence that you can do it and take those first few struggling steps. Only you can do it; no one can do it for you. Are you afraid of what is around the corner, afraid of what the future holds? Where are your faith and trust? Why not learn to live fully and gloriously in the ever-present now, and let Me look after the future for you? I have wonderful things waiting for you when you are free and cease to cling to what you already have because you are afraid of losing everything. Be willing to lose everything to gain something far, far greater. All is in My hands, and all is very, very well.

*L*IFE is simple! Why make it complicated for yourself? Why choose the devious path when the straight path lies before you? Let life unfold for you, and do not try to force its unfoldment. You cannot force the unfolding of a flower, for if you try to do so, you will destroy the beauty and perfection of that flower by your impatience. There is a right time for everything, so why not get into rhythm with life, flow with it and behold My wonders and glories unfold in true perfection? When something is done out of timing, it holds up so much, instead of speeding it along, as may be imagined. Therefore wait upon Me in quietness and confidence, and never try to rush ahead and do something out of timing. At the same time never drag your feet and waste precious time. Realise that there is a glorious pattern and plan running through everything you do, and give eternal thanks.

THE primary lesson to learn in life is to love. Love is so strong that it is unbreakable, and yet it is intangible. You can know it; you can feel it; and yet you cannot hold on to it; for as soon as you try, it will slip away like quicksilver. Love cannot be possessed; it is as free as the wind and moves where it will. Move with it. Love is unity and wholeness. Love knows no limitation, no barriers. With love comes freedom. It is fear that binds and limits a soul; it is love that frees and cuts away all bonds. Love opens all doors, changes lives and melts the hardest of hearts. Love is creative; it builds up, creating beauty, harmony and oneness. It works for, not against, anything. Love brings such joy that it cannot be repressed. It dances and sings through life. Is there love in your heart? Love for each other? It starts in you and works out and out.

DO you feel that you are part of the new? Do you feel that you blend in with the whole in perfect harmony, or do you feel uncomfortable and ill at ease? If you do, it is far better to move out and find another way. Only those souls who are in harmony with the new, who are willing to leave all the old behind without any regrets and who have the spirit of adventure, are ready for the new and will be able to move freely into it. If you still want to hold on to the old orthodox and conventional ways and ideas, afraid to break the old moulds, then you are not ready for the new. It takes courage, strength, determination and a deep inner knowing that what you are doing is right. When your faith and trust are in Me and you know that I AM guiding and directing you, you will be able to do all that needs to be done with deepest love and joy.

USE all you have for the benefit of the whole. Do not try to accumulate or hoard it, but share it; for as you share, so will it grow; whereas if you try to hold on and possess something or someone, you will surely lose it. It is the law, and as you live it, you will see it working out all around you. If you have some packets of seeds and you put them away in a cupboard and forget about them, nothing will happen to them, and there they will remain. But if you take them and plant them in the ground and tend them, they will not only grow but will accumulate and produce more and more. So with all you have: never try to cling on to it but gladly share it, and watch it grow and grow in quantity and quality. When your attitude is right, you know that all your needs are being wonderfully met, and that all I have is yours.

T is not necessary for you to try and work things out in life yourself, or try to pull strings. All you have to do is very quietly and confidently to follow My instructions which you will receive in the stillness. Some souls will hear My voice distinctly; others will act intuitively; some souls will be guided in action. I work in many ways, but all will know when I AM in command, for the hallmarks of love and truth will be running through everything. As My instructions are obeyed, you will behold wonder upon wonder take place and see My hand in everything. You will realise that of yourself you could not bring these wonders about and that it is indeed I working in you, and you will give Me the honour and glory and eternal thanks. Acknowledge at all times where your wisdom, love and understanding come from, where life itself comes from. I AM the Allness of All, and your life is hid in Me. We are one.

E at peace and rest in My love. You have heard these words many times, and you wonder why they have to be repeated. They are like water: very slowly and silently they wear away the old and find a new way. They go on and on, gradually sinking deeper and deeper within you until you find they have become a part of you. They are no longer just words, but they live and move and have their being in you, and you find yourself living them and at perfect peace resting in My love. Never resent repetition, but be eternally grateful that My love is so great that I AM willing patiently and persistently to go on and will never let you go. I have placed My hand upon you, and I have need of you. You have a very special place in My vast overall plan, and I AM waiting to reveal it to you when you are ready.

*Y*OU will never know whether something works unless you try it. You will never know whether the electricity is on unless you put your hand on the switch and switch it on; you have to take some action to prove that it works. So with faith. It is useless just sitting there talking about faith if you do not live by it and if no one can see what it means to you. It is useless talking about living by faith when your security is in your bank balance, and you know you can draw on it whenever you choose to do so. It is when you have nothing and can step off the deep end and do the seemingly impossible because your faith and security are rooted and grounded in Me, that you can talk about living by faith and be a living demonstration of it. Go ahead and put your faith to the test and see what happens!

LWAYS see the bright side of life. Expect only the very best to come about, and see it do so. Never blame anyone else for the negative state you are in. You are your own master; it is up to you to reverse the picture and see what is on the other side. If you choose to see the gloomy side of life, do not expect to draw to you those souls who know the joy of true freedom, for like attracts like; you will draw to you only those souls who are in the same state. When you are on top of the world and love is flowing freely from you, you will draw all, for everyone enjoys a joyful soul. Learn to lift a person or a situation, and never allow yourself to be dragged down into the depths of despair by anyone else's attitude. You are here to create peace, harmony, beauty and perfection, all the very best in life, so get on and do something about it!

WHEN I say to you, 'Love one another,' it does not mean that you are to tolerate one another, or to try very hard to love one another. But you will find when you open your heart and can fill it with loving, beautiful thoughts that you will want to love all those souls you come into contact with, no matter who they are. It is the free flow of My universal love which knows no discrimination, and does not pick and choose who is going to be loved and who is not. My love is the same for each and every one. How much of it you are willing to accept is up to you. Be not afraid to express this love. It is beyond the personality; it is of the very highest. Learn to wear your heart on your sleeve, and never be ashamed to demonstrate your love for one another. Love is the greatest uniting factor in the universe, so love, love, love.

BY their fruits ye shall know them,' whether they are for Me or against Me, whether they are of the light or of the darkness. Open your eyes and you will know with no uncertain knowing. Go within and your heart will tell you. Do your own assessing and do not listen to everything without; for if you listen to the many whisperings and rumours without, you will find yourself in such a quandary that you will not know what is the truth and what is not, and you will lose your way. All souls can find the truth within, but it does mean they have to take time to go within. They have to do their own thinking and find their own way, and many souls are too lazy to do it. They find it so much easier to listen to what others say and to accept what is said without going within. Be still and you will know the truth; and the truth shall set you free.

HERE is no need for suffering in the New Age. For those souls who are moving into the new, suffering is no more. If you still feel that suffering is necessary, you are not of the new, but are firmly stuck in the old. There you will remain, drawing suffering to yourself until of your own free will you move on and accept that it is no more. Concentrate on the wonders and joys of this life, and accept the very best which is your true heritage. It is not being an ostrich, afraid of life and not facing it. It is seeing the reality of this glorious life which is yours and, in doing so, helping to bring it about. The more clearly you can see it, the more quickly will it come about. Accept the vision of the new heaven and new earth, and hold it ever in your consciousness, for it is no unattainable dream. It is reality, and you are part of it.

*T*HERE is a great need for stable and dependable souls, ones who are always in the right place at the right time doing what needs to be done. There is a need for souls living in such a way that nothing upsets them, because they are in complete control of every situation and live and act from that inner centre of peace and stillness. Their security is in Me; therefore nothing can throw them off balance. They know what they are doing and why they are doing it, and they have a real sense of responsibility. They can be completely depended upon to see a job through, no matter what it is, and see it through perfectly. Search your heart. Are you dependable? Have you a sense of responsibility so that you see a job through to the end? Are you always in the right place at the right time? It is important that you take time to see where you are missing out, and then see what you can do to rectify it.

HAVE love and confidence in one another, for love and confidence in a soul enable it to flower and develop, so it can take on responsibilities and grow in strength and stature. You cannot expect a child to grow in stature if everything is done for it. It has to be taught to think for itself, to make its own decisions and not rely on its parents to do all its thinking for it. It is not easy to see loved ones making the wrong decision, and yet at times it has to be done, so that they learn certain lessons. Lessons can be learnt the easy way, but often when they are learnt the hard way they are never forgotten. So never be over-protective; learn to take your hands off those souls under your care, no matter who they are or what age. Let them learn to shoulder their responsibilities and, what is more, to enjoy doing so, and help each other to grow.

ODAY is a new day, and it is up to you what you make of it. Your first waking thoughts can colour the whole day. They can be happy, positive thoughts or miserable, negative ones. Never be influenced by outer conditions—by the weather, for example. It can be pouring with rain, but if your heart is filled with love and gratitude, your whole attitude will be of sunshine and blue skies. Do you see what a tremendous responsibility rests upon your shoulders? Life is what you make it, so never blame anyone else for the state you are in, but know that it is of your own making. Change your attitude and you can change your whole outlook. Adopt a constructive attitude towards life. Build up the very best from what you see all around you, and ignore the rest; give it no life force and it will disappear. Wait upon Me this day in quietness and confidence, and know that this day has My blessings.

WHAT are your values in life? If they are simply the material ones which are here today and gone tomorrow, you can spend your life rushing around like a squirrel in a cage getting nowhere. But if you seek the ways of the Spirit, you need to seek within to find them, and it can only be done by being still and drawing forth those priceless treasures which are deep within you. You will not find them without, for you contain within you all that matters in life. You are free to make your own choice regarding the things that matter. No one is going to try and influence you, for every soul has free will. It is up to you whether you make a mess of your life or a success of it. The light is there; why not follow it? The love is there; why not accept it? Nothing is withheld from you when you seek for it with your whole heart, mind, soul and strength.

*Y*OU cannot move on to greater works until you have sorted out your relationships, and walk in love, peace and harmony with each other, harbouring no resentments or ill will. Weeds have to be plucked from the ground before they choke the plants which are growing there. Pluck out all the weeds in your life now, before they become firmly established and suffocate those beautiful plants which are growing within you. You cannot grow and expand spiritually when you harbour any hate, jealousy, dislike, intolerance or misunderstanding in your heart. Sort out your differences quickly and keep the love flowing. Never wait for the other person to make the first move. You can always do something about it, so why not do it and do it now? Never put off until tomorrow what can be done today. Much is waiting to unfold, but it must unfold in the right atmosphere, the atmosphere of love, love and more love.

I was shown a great ball of light. Coming from it were bright rays of light and going back into it were very dull rays. I heard the words:

When you have been the full cycle, you will return to Me, the source of all life, and you will become one with Me as you were in the beginning.

LEAVE yesterday behind and move swiftly into this wonderful new day, knowing that it holds within it only the very best for you, and expect only the very best to come out of it. See My hand in all that is taking place, and behold the birth of the new heaven and new earth. Fear not, for it is My good pleasure to give you the kingdom, not tomorrow or some time, but today. Can you accept that anything can happen today? Are you prepared for the most wonderful happenings to take place? It helps to hasten things on and enables you to see only the very best come out of every situation. In fact, because you are looking for the very best, you help to bring it about. By this very positive action you create the right conditions, the right environment for the unfolding of the new. You become like a midwife, ready to assist in every way to bring it forth.

IONEERS are always needed, those souls who have the strength and courage to forge ahead into the new. They are the ones who have vision and who hold that vision ever before them and see it unfold. But everyone is an individual and therefore cannot be placed in a mould. You must be free to grow and develop and be inspired by those deep inner promptings which stir and move your very being. Live by the Spirit; act by the promptings of the Spirit, no matter how foolish those promptings may appear to be. It is far more comfortable to sit back and wait for someone else to make the first move, to take that leap into the unknown. It takes faith and courage to be able to do it; and if you have not the faith and courage to do it, do not try to hold back or stop those pioneers who have. But be eternally grateful, for without them My new heaven and new earth could never be established.

OU are part of the whole, and each soul has its part to play in the whole. So be not critical or intolerant of one another, but realise that no two of you are the same and that it takes many different parts to make up the perfect whole. Have you ever seen a clock taken to pieces? There are many different parts that make up that clock, and as you see them lying there before you, you wonder how they could ever make up a perfect timepiece. But when someone who knows something about clocks takes each piece and puts it in its rightful place, you find that not only does it go, but it tells the correct time. As long as each tiny piece remains in its rightful place, playing its part, everything goes smoothly. Now you know why I keep telling you to find your rightful place in the whole vast scheme of life, and when you have found it, to give of your very best.

EARN to appreciate and care for all that is given to you. You will only do it when you realise that all you have comes from Me. When you truly love the giver, you will cherish the gift. When you fail to look after My gifts, it reflects your attitude towards Me, the giver of all those gifts. Love is the key. When you know the meaning of love, you will never fail to love and care for all that is put in your charge. You do not give a child a valuable piece of equipment to play with because you know that child will not look after it and will probably destroy it. I cannot give you all that is waiting to be given to you until you learn to look after it and use it the way it should be used, with love and care. Therefore I have to wait patiently until you are ready before I can give you more and more of My gifts.

WHY go around with your eyes shut and your mind closed, and so fail to recognise your true heritage? Realise that you do not have to search without for wisdom, knowledge and understanding; it is all there within you, waiting to be drawn out. When you become aware of it, you will never again feel that one soul is more intelligent than another. You will know that as souls become aware that they contain all deep within them, they will be able to do all things and understand all things; in fact a whole new world will open up for them. You are a world unto yourself, a world that contains all light, love, wisdom, truth and understanding, waiting to be drawn out. So cease searching for it from without. Take time to be still and find it within you. Learn to understand yourself, and as you do, you will begin to understand others, to understand life, to understand Me.

*L*ET neither intellectual pride nor preconceived ideas, opinions and prejudices lock and bar the way; nor close yourself to truth because it does not come through conventional or orthodox means. You are moving into the new, and therefore you must be prepared for many new ways and means. When a child is moved into a higher grade in school, it has to learn to expand and to take in and accept all the new subjects it has to learn. So it is with moving into the New Age. You have to be willing to branch out, to try new experiments, to step out into the unknown. You even have to be willing to make mistakes and learn by those mistakes, knowing that as you do so, you will keep growing in wisdom and knowledge and understanding. Do not be concerned; you will not be moved up from the first grade straight into the sixth grade. Step by step the way will be revealed to you, and you will be moved gradually.

WHEN you are out of harmony with the divine order of things, you draw to you disharmony and disunity. You will find yourself swimming against the tide, getting nowhere and simply exhausting yourself. Why not go with the tide, flow along with it and get into harmony with what is going on? As you learn to do it, you will find yourself in harmony with everything and everyone around you. You will no longer stick out like a sore thumb, but will blend in perfectly with your surroundings and environment. You will find you are in harmony with yourself, and that harmony within will be reflected without. Life will flow smoothly and all will fall into place perfectly. You will behold seeming miracle upon miracle come about all the time. This way of living will become the normal way with you because you are in tune with Me and I can work in and through you to bring about My wonders and glories.

OW many times during the day are you consciously aware of Me? How many times during the day do you recognise My hand in what is happening and give Me thanks? Take time today and try to keep in contact with Me all the time. You will not find it easy to begin with, for you will find yourself wandering off through the highways and byways of life when not one single thought of Me enters your consciousness for long periods of time. To begin with you will have to learn to bring your consciousness back to Me and to stop it wandering aimlessly. But as you keep on doing it, gradually you will become more and more consciously aware of Me. You will learn to live and move and have your being in Me, and you will know the meaning of our oneness: that there is no separation, that I AM in you and you are in Me, and that we are one.

*T*O set the pace for the day, you have to learn to be still and have a time of attunement in the early morning on waking, before your mind becomes embroiled with all the events of the day. Your life is like a clean canvas without a mark on it. Let those first strokes on waking be very clear and definite. Let them be full of love, inspiration and expectation of the very best for the new day ahead of you. You will find yourself in a very quiet, receptive and impressionable state. In that state you will be able to direct the activities of your mind along the highest and most desirable path. Enter the new day prepared for the very best to take place in everything you undertake. Step by step see the perfect pattern unfold for the day and for you. Yesterday is behind you, a new and glorious day is before you, and you are in harmony with all life.

D O not waste time and energy thrashing around like a fish out of water, blaming your conditions and circumstances on somebody else. Simply know that it is all in your hands. Therefore you can rectify it yourself without any help from anyone else when you take the time to find inner peace and stillness and wait upon Me. Nothing will be hidden from you when you seek it and when you lay all before Me and seek to do My will and My will alone. You will only find what My will is when you learn to be still. Do not try too hard; let go, relax and find that peace of heart and mind which opens all doors and reveals the light of truth. You will find you will achieve far more when you can relax and put everything into My hands. Then very quietly wait upon Me and allow things to flow freely and naturally without any effort on your part, and so unfold in true perfection.

THE best way to bring love and prosperity into your life is to bless everything and give thanks for every increase which comes your way as a gift from Me. As you learn to bless and give thanks for everything, you are actually putting into practice one of the great laws of prosperity and plenty, for with love and blessings comes increase. You have seen a child expand and grow in beauty and wisdom when love and blessings are poured down upon it. You have seen plants and flowers and animals respond to love and blessings. You have felt yourself respond when love and blessings are poured down upon you. Now go and do likewise to everyone you contact. You will find the more you do it, the easier it becomes, and the more easily you can open your heart, until love and blessings flow from you all the time and the very joy of living is bubbling over in you out into the world.

WHEN you realise the hours of practice a good pianist has to put in each day before performing a superb concert, you will begin to understand why you have to keep ever on the alert to be able to live this spiritual life the way it should be lived. It does not mean you have to strain, but it does mean you have to be constantly on the alert and aware of what is happening, especially at first. Like the pianist practising for perfection having to go over and over a certain difficult piece before reaching a feeling of satisfaction, so do you have to go over and over the same ground, learning the same lessons until they have become so much a part of you that you cannot separate yourself from them, for they are ingrained. Remember, no one else can live this life for you; no one else can do your practising for you. Only you can do it. So why not start doing it now?

IT is when I can work in and through open and willing channels that amazing happenings can come about. All those souls who see them come about can see My hand in them and realise that of themselves they would be incapable of doing them. They know that I AM indeed working in and through them, and in this way they come to know Me and to love Me. Therefore never fail to give thanks for everything that is taking place in your life. Keep your heart open and your mind uncluttered by negative thoughts so that no time need be wasted clearing away old thought forms which can hold up the progress of the new. Always remember that simplicity is My hallmark. Therefore when life becomes too complicated for you, you may be sure you are off beam and need to get back on to it as quickly as possible. Be like a little child, simple and uncomplicated, and enjoy life to the full.

HOLD in your consciousness that good comes out of everything and that every experience is given to you to help you to grow and expand. Realise that without first-hand experience you would not be able to understand or open your heart to your fellow human beings, but would stand aloof and even judge and condemn. Experiences, no matter how strange or difficult, have been given to you for a purpose; therefore take the time to look for that purpose. Try to see My hand in everything, to see that nothing is by chance, and that there is no such thing as luck or good fortune. Realise that you draw to yourself all the very best or the very worst in life. It can be peace, serenity and tranquillity, or it can be chaos and confusion. It comes from within, from your state of consciousness; therefore do not blame your surroundings. A snail carries its all with it, even its house. You carry all within, and it is reflected without.

HE divine spark is within each individual, but it needs to be drawn out and fanned into a flame in many souls. Wake up from your slumbers, recognise the divinity within you, and nurture it and allow it to grow and flourish. A seed has to be planted in the soil before it can grow. It has within it all its potential, but that potential remains dormant until given the right conditions in which to grow and develop. You have within you the kingdom of heaven, but unless you wake up to the fact and start searching for it, you will not find it, and there it will remain. There are many souls in this life who will not wake up to this fact, and they are like seeds stored away in packets. You must want to break your bonds to be free. As soon as the desire is there, you will receive help in every way possible. But the desire in you must be there first.

E ye transformed by the renewing of your mind.' How important these words are! You have heard them many times, but what have you done about them? What do they mean to you? Take time to ponder on them until they become living, vibrating words in your life and you do feel yourself being transformed by the renewing of your mind. You talk of peace and harmony, of the new heaven and new earth, of doing My will, of love and light being radiated out into the world and of moving into the new, but what are you actually doing about it? Are you living in such a way that you are helping to bring it all about? Don't allow yourself to become like a parrot, saying things that mean nothing to you. Pray without ceasing for deeper and clearer understanding, and give thanks and move forward and upward. Above all, live a life and let things happen to transform your life.

WHEN you are in contact with Me and your greatest desire is to do My will, you will find that every action you take must be done not for the self but for the good of the whole. This life is only for completely dedicated souls who are willing to leave the self behind and become part of the whole. It is not easy for the majority of humanity to do, for many souls are not willing to give up their individuality. They want to cling on to what they call their 'rights', and do exactly what they want to do, without consideration for anyone else. Therefore, if ever you feel that life is not going your way and you are out of harmony with the whole, take time to find out what it is within you that is causing the disharmony, and never look around for a scapegoat you can blame. When you realise it is something within yourself that is causing it, you can rectify it without delay.

EASE straining after anything and simply allow things to unfold. Do not allow worry to bind you and blind you, but learn to cast all your burdens upon Me so that you are free to do My will and walk in My ways. I cannot use you when you are tied up with yourself and cannot see the wood for the trees, so relax and let go. Be still and dwell on the wonders of life. Let your mind be stayed on Me. Open your eyes and see Me in everything, and give eternal thanks. When you can see Me in everything, your heart is so full you cannot fail to give thanks; it simply bubbles up in you and flows out. You cannot hide a heart full of love and gratitude, for it is reflected for all to see. When you are in a state of joy and thanksgiving, you attract others to you. Everyone enjoys being with a soul who overflows with love, for love attracts love.

*T*HIS is a life of action, a life of change. Let there be no complacency, for when you are complacent, you can so easily get into a rut which creates stagnation. You have to do your own spiritual work. You have to do your own searching in your own way. See where you need to change and then take the action necessary to bring about that change. If change is uncomfortable, the more quickly it takes place, the easier it is. It is far less painful to pull a bandage off quickly than to do it slowly. Therefore do what you know has to be done without wasting any time thinking about it. Take that leap into the new without hesitation, and simply know it will be far more wonderful than what you have left behind in the old. With change comes life, a full and glorious life. It is being held out to you. Take it and give eternal thanks for it.

SEEK ye first the kingdom, put Me first in everything and then all else shall be added unto you. You know these words, but what are you doing about them? Are you living them? Do the ways of the Spirit come first in your life? Does your time alone with Me mean more to you than anything? Do you enjoy being still, or are you uncomfortable and uneasy in the stillness? Do you always want to be busy doing things and find great difficulty in stilling your body and mind? There are millions of souls in the world who cannot bear to have silence. They have to have constant noise and action around them. They are the ones who do not know the meaning of seeking first My kingdom and of putting Me first in their lives. They are restless within and without. I tell you, the times of peace and stillness when we are together are very precious in a world of turmoil. Seek them, find them and remain in them.

*L*EARN to live beyond yourself and your own strength and ability, so that those people around you can see with their own eyes that it is I working in and through you. In this way, those souls who have no faith and belief will come to know Me, not by many words, but by a life direct and demonstrated. Unless you live in this way, you are not acknowledging that I AM your guide and companion and that you have dedicated your life completely to Me and to My service. You have to take your feet off the bottom and swim out into the deep unknown in absolute faith and confidence, knowing that no harm will befall you because I AM with you. You will never know whether it all is so unless you are willing to do something about it. Cease playing safe, and let Me show you what can happen when you let go and allow Me to take over and use you as I will.

'AS you give, so shall you receive.' These are not just words; they are the law. As you live them and put them into action, you will see how wonderfully they work. You will find as you start giving that which you have, so will more and more be given you. Fear nothing, withhold nothing; simply give and go on giving. An open, generous heart draws all the very best to it. Let your heart be open and generous so that you withhold nothing, and let the spirit of giving be ever there. Assess what you have to give and then give it, no matter what it is, for as each gift is offered, it helps to complete the whole. Do not expect someone else to draw your gifts out of you, but give willingly of what you have. As you do, you will see where it fits into the whole, as the piece of a jigsaw puzzle when placed in its rightful position completes the picture.

GIVE Me the opportunity to work in and through you to bring about My wonders and glories. Hold the vision of My limitless love ever before you, of My limitless abundance and of My wonders and glories coming about. Hold the vision of the new heaven and new earth, of My will being done, and of peace and harmony on earth and good will towards all. Hold the vision of vast cities of light springing up all over the world where peace and love reign supreme. Never at any time lose the vision, for it is by holding the vision firmly and clearly ever before you that you help to bring it down from the etheric, and see these wonders manifest on the earth plane for all to behold. The clearer the vision, the quicker will it be manifested. Give constant thanks that your eyes have been opened and that you know what to do. Now go ahead and do it, and stop thinking about it!

HE speed with which changes can unfold will astound you. You have been prepared for these changes for a long time. Through the ages, day by day, month by month, year by year, I have very patiently set the scene for these changes to take place. You have been given every opportunity to adjust and prepare yourself; therefore you should be able to move forward without any difficulty. It is a question of consciousness, of being able to raise your consciousness and adjust to all that is taking place. Those souls who are aware of the Christ consciousness are being drawn together at this time like steel to a magnet. They may not always be aware of it at the time, but it will become very clear to them in the days ahead. It is this consciousness which is drawing more and more souls together so that you all may become aware of the Christ within, and give eternal thanks for this awareness.

DAY by day you become more and more infilled and infused with the Christ consciousness. You are able to walk in the light and become one with the light until there is no darkness in you, and as this process takes place you bring more light into the world. You must realise that it all starts in you. You have to put your own house in order first, and you must have the faith and confidence that you can do so and then do it. It is what is within you that is reflected without. It is not something to be striven for; it is something that just happens if only you will let it, and fill your heart and mind with love and understanding. This raised state of consciousness is in the very air you breathe. Breathe it in deeply and let your whole being be infilled with it. It is so great that you cannot contain it; therefore breathe it out, and so keep it moving and growing.

WHAT do you expect from life? Do you expect the very best, or are you one of those souls who is always afraid the worst is going to happen, that things will go wrong? If you are, you deserve what is coming to you, for you attract to you that which you love or that which you hate and fear. When your consciousness is negative, you draw negativity towards you like steel to a magnet, and you will find yourself keeping company with those souls of like mind, for like attracts like. When your consciousness is of love, when you are bubbling over with the joys of life and when your heart is filled with gratitude for everyone and everything, you will find yourself drawing towards you those happy, joyful souls who radiate love and joy wherever they go. Your life will be filled with the very best life can offer. Why not see the very best in every situation? See the very best being drawn to you now.

ANY times you may have to go ahead in faith, unable to see the full reason for the action you are taking, but do not hesitate when you know within that it is right. You must have faith to be able to take steps into the unknown, for there may be many outer influences pulling you this way and that until you feel torn to pieces. This is where you have to learn to go within and know with absolute knowing that what you are doing is being guided by Me and will work out perfectly. It takes great faith and courage to step out and follow those deep inner promptings, especially when the action you are taking appears as utter foolishness in the eyes of others. That is why you could not do it without complete faith and inner knowing. The choice always lies in your hands; therefore choose and choose aright with your hand firmly in Mine. I will never fail you or forsake you, but will guide your every step.

ET there be unity in diversity. See the many paths all leading to the centre, to Me, each one different and yet each one leading in the same direction. The closer they come to the centre, the greater the unity, until all become one in Me and there is no longer diversity but complete unity. You will find it taking place more and more with the many centres of light all over the world. As the world situation grows darker and worsens, so shall they grow brighter and brighter, until light overcomes all darkness. It is good to see a wider picture of what is taking place, but it is also very important to realise that it all starts within you. Realise that what is taking place within the individual goes out into the world and is reflected in the world situation. That is why peace of heart and mind is so essential within you, and why harmony, understanding and deep love should flow between you and all others.

OPEN your heart and accept all My good and perfect gifts. They are there waiting for you, but many souls fail to open their hearts and stretch forth their hands to accept their rightful heritage. They are either afraid to do so, or feel they are unworthy, or simply do not believe that it is there, and therefore reject what is waiting for them to claim. When you have money in the bank but refuse to accept that it is there and refuse to draw from that supply because of your disbelief, you are the one who suffers lack and has to do without. My storehouses are full to overflowing, and all that I have is yours; but you have to do something about it; you have to claim what is yours. You cannot live this spiritual life unless you believe that it is yours and claim it. The new heaven and new earth are here now.

OU are My hands and feet. I have to work in and through you to reveal My wonders and glories. I have to use you to bring down My kingdom, to bring about the new heaven and new earth. Until you become aware that I have need of you, you will go on hearing about this wonderful new heaven and new earth, but you will not behold it, live in it and see it working in and all around you. What is the use of a dream of Utopia? It has to be made reality, and it can only happen when you start to live it and stop talking about it. If you see a person drowning, it is not much help shouting instructions from the shore. You have to jump in and do something to help. Therefore there is not much use in reading about how to create the new heaven and new earth or learning about it. You have to start living it now to bring it about.

ONCE you have taken a step forward in faith, never look backwards or start regretting what you have left behind. Simply expect the most wonderful future and see it come about. Leave all the old behind; it is finished. Be grateful for the lessons you have learnt and for the experiences you have had, which have all helped you to grow and have given you a deeper understanding, but never try to cling on to them. What is waiting for you is far, far more wonderful than what you have left behind. When you have placed your life under My direct guidance and direction, how can anything go wrong? It is when you have taken a step forward and then wonder if you have done right, and you allow doubts and fears in, that things begin to crowd in on you, and you find yourself bowed down by the weight of your decision. Therefore let go, release the past and move forward with your heart filled with love and gratitude.

Eileen Caddy, who is the co-founder of the Findhorn Foundation and Community in the north of Scotland, has based her life on obeying her 'still small voice within'. Since 1962, when she and her husband Peter and their three small children were led to Findhorn Bay Caravan Park, thousands of people have been attracted to visit and many have remained to create a community based on spiritual principles and co-operation with the nature kingdoms.

Today the community is a vibrant, challenging and expanding place, with around 500 people actively involved in some way with its inner and outer work. It is possible for guests to visit and participate in the day-to-day life or in the many workshops offered by the Findhorn Foundation. For further details please write to The Accommodation Secretary, Findhorn Foundation, Cluny Hill College, Forres, Scotland IV36 0RD.